REVERSE
MENTORING

REVERSE MENTORING

REMOVING BARRIERS AND
BUILDING BELONGING
IN THE WORKPLACE

Patrice Gordon

hachette
BOOKS

NEW YORK

Copyright © 2022 by Patrice Gordon

Cover design by Sara Pinsonault
Cover copyright © 2022 by Hachette Book Group, Inc.

Hachette Go, an imprint of Hachette Books
Hachette Book Group
1290 Avenue of the Americas
New York, NY 10104
HachetteGo.com
Facebook.com/HachetteGo
Instagram.com/HachetteGo

First Edition: November 2022

Hachette Books is a division of Hachette Book Group, Inc.

The Hachette Go and Hachette Books names and logos are trademarks of Hachette Book Group, Inc.

Print book interior design by Linda Mark.

Library of Congress Cataloging-in-Publication Data
Names: Gordon, Patrice L., author.
Title: Reverse mentoring: removing barriers and building belonging in the
  workplace / Patrice Gordon.
Description: New York, NY: Hachette Go, an imprint of Hachette Books, [2022]
Identifiers: LCCN 2022019106 | ISBN 9780306829611 (hardcover) |
  ISBN 9780306829628 (paperback) | ISBN 9780306829635 (ebook)
Subjects: LCSH: Employees—Coaching of. | Diversity in the Workplace—
  Management. | Personnel management. | Interpersonal relations. | Leadership.
Classification: LCC HF5549.5.C53 G667 2022 | DDC
658.3/124—dc23/eng/20220707
LC record available at https://lccn.loc.gov/2022019106

ISBNs: 978-0-306-82961-1 (hardcover); 978-0-306-82963-5 (ebook)

Printed in the United States of America

LSC-C

Printing 1, 2022

Dedicated to those underrepresented voices everywhere.

I pray I have conveyed your stories with clarity and conviction.

May I continue to use my voice as a force for good.

In loving memory of Sarah.

Contents

Foreword

HOLLY BRANSON

I learned so much from Patrice Gordon's wonderful book: *Reverse Mentoring: Removing Barriers and Building Belonging in the Workplace*. As chief purpose and vision officer of Virgin Group, I am passionate that not only our businesses but *all* businesses become truly diverse, inclusive, and equitable, and I strive to be as educated and informed as I can be, to help make this a reality.

What I love about Patrice's book is that she continually brings us back to the fact that a workplace is made up of people—not robots. Yes, many of those people will share the same skill sets, but they will undoubtedly have had different lived experiences and face different challenges. The joy and success of a work culture where everyone feels that they belong, have a shared purpose, and are respected and valued equally to their colleagues, regardless of their gender, ethnicity, neurodiversity, disabilities, or socioeconomic background, should never be underestimated.

A business that works hard to foster a sense of true belonging and inclusion for all of its people has been shown to be substantially more successful than those businesses that simply pay lip service to diversity, equity, and inclusion. I'm continually shouting from the rooftops that: "Purpose and profit go hand in hand"—because I absolutely believe that they do! To be a truly purpose-led business (and therefore a successful one!), your people and their well-being should be at the heart of everything you do. The issue comes when leaders don't actually know who their people are.

Leadership teams everywhere will learn much from Patrice's book. As she so brilliantly puts it:

> Change does not happen with a one-off diversity training or listening session. It does not happen because your organization hires more people of color or promotes more women to leadership positions. It does not happen because of an anti-discrimination policy codified by lawyers and printed in the employee handbook. It happens when people—real people with all their flaws and attributes—change from the inside out. If we want to promote this kind of change, we need a tool that promotes dialogue, connection, empathy, and vulnerability between multiple parties that allows people from dispa-

rate backgrounds to truly engage with and understand one another. Enter reverse mentoring.

Without taking the time to get to know your colleagues' lived experiences, the challenges they face, their personal and family journeys, their fears, their skills, and their passions, you will never bring out the best in your people. And, crucially, you will never break down those barriers, conscious or unconscious, that prevent even the most well-intentioned businesses from becoming 100 percent diverse, inclusive, and equitable. Breaking down these barriers, at all levels of your organization, will shine a light on a richer, more engaged talent pool; it will encourage creative, lively debate that often leads to accelerated innovation; and you'll become an organization that encourages, values, respects, and promotes all the amazing skills already available to you—within your own people. People whom you have taken the time to get to know. As an added bonus you, as a leader, will also get to understand better what makes you tick and how you can grow as an employer and as a person—opening up so many more opportunities to thrive, in both work and life.

Reverse Mentoring: Removing Barriers and Building Belonging in the Workplace is an inspiring how-to when it comes to all aspects of introducing a successful reverse mentoring program. Patrice takes you through every element, step by step, in such a warm and human way that I forgot at times I was reading a business book. Reading the last chapter, you can't help but get excited about what the future will look like if all businesses embrace Patrice's passion for reverse mentorship; her passion for a world in which all businesses are 100 percent diverse, inclusive, and equitable shines through on every page.

It's only right to give the wonderful Patrice the last word:

> By using our own stories to bring more humanity into our organizations, reverse mentoring allows us to see one another and ourselves in a radically new light. Only when we look at the world differently can we decide to make change—change that, in this case, is long overdue and sorely needed. Let's begin.

REVERSE
MENTORING

CHAPTER ONE

WHY REVERSE MENTORING MATTERS NOW

When I was eleven years old, my mother enrolled me in an all-girls Catholic school on the outskirts of London. Out of roughly 200 students in my grade, I was one of just nine Black girls.

The school curriculum was structured around different levels for different subjects. If you showed particular aptitude in a certain subject, you could move up to a more rigorous level and further develop your skills. Most of the time this happened automatically: a teacher would notice an above-average student and recommend them for advancement.

I had never considered myself especially gifted academically, so I was pleasantly surprised when I started testing consistently well in mathematics. I found that I enjoyed the logic and structure of numbers and had a natural aptitude for solving complex equations and problems. Yet despite

1

earning grades that should have qualified me for the highest mathematics level, none of my teachers recommended me. It was as though, to them—the same people who were instructing and evaluating me every day—I was somehow invisible. Finally, I reached out to one of my teachers, Ms. Rodriguez, whom I still remember fondly, and asked what I needed to do to move up. She offered me extra instruction during my lunch breaks, and, eventually, I advanced.

At the time, it did not occur to me that my teachers' lack of attention had anything to do with my race. Like many people of color and children of immigrants (my parents and I had emigrated from Jamaica when I was three years old), I'd learned from a young age that it was better to put my head down and work hard rather than draw even more attention to my already-obvious differences. Still, I was frustrated that I had to work harder than most of my peers for my teachers to notice my talent.

When I was sixteen, I told my mother that I wanted to transfer to a public college (the UK equivalent of high school) in South London that was much more diverse. Though the school had an excellent track record of getting students into university, it was much rougher around the edges than my previous one. Students frequently got into fights, and a security guard was stationed at the main entrance. Even though my mother was apprehensive, she relented because we both knew, deep down, that I would thrive more in a place where I felt that I belonged.

Our instincts were right. Not only did my teachers at the new school notice my talents, but they were the first people to tell me that I should apply to university—a reality I had never considered, let alone planned for. As a result of their care, attention, and validation, I became the first person in my family to attend and graduate from university. I've always been proud of this accomplishment, of course, but I never fully appreciated the lessons I took away from my primary school experience until much later when I was well into my career.

One day in mid-2018, after more than a decade of working in finance for large national and multinational corporations, I was speaking with my colleague Estelle when she mentioned an interesting opportunity. Estelle and I both worked at Virgin Atlantic, where she was vice president of people experience and I served as head of commercial finance. Estelle and I had joined the company at around the same time, and I immediately clicked with her. Even though I had worked in finance for my entire career, I'd always been interested in personal and professional development and creating change within organizations. After training as an executive coach and gaining a post-graduate qualification in coaching, I set up a coaching consultancy firm to help individuals, particularly women, develop their skills and succeed.

"We're looking for someone to mentor Craig, and I thought of you." Estelle said. "Would you be interested?"

Craig Kreeger was CEO of Virgin Atlantic at the time and his career in the airline industry spanned more than three decades. Although I was relatively senior within the organization, I was several levels below the C-suite and several decades younger than Craig. Why would he need me to mentor him?

Estelle explained that the idea was part of the company's "Be Yourself" program, a recent initiative designed to encourage employees to bring their whole, authentic selves to work. The leadership team had realized that this may be easier said than done for employees from traditionally marginalized groups in a company that was run predominantly by white men. Perhaps by actively encouraging senior leaders to interact with and learn more about colleagues with different lived experiences, they might foster a more inclusive environment from the top down.

Craig had volunteered to be partnered with a more junior colleague and requested a Black female mentor because there were no Black women in his professional or social circles. Because I was a valued member of the team who had consistently expressed interest in helping drive change at the company, Estelle had tapped me for the opportunity. I agreed.

Over the next six months, Craig and I met one-on-one and in private for an hour every four to six weeks. I told him about my childhood and what it was like working in a field where I was often the only woman *and* person of color in the room. I told him the story about my primary school experience and how, looking back, it was apparent that my teachers had dismissed my potential based on the color of my skin. When he asked what my experience had been like at Virgin Atlantic, I was honest. I explained that I would have liked to see more diversity at senior levels. He listened attentively, acknowledged some of the company's gaps, and agreed that though Virgin Atlantic was in a good state, good wasn't good enough. He also opened up about his own experiences growing up the son of Jewish Israeli immigrants in the United States and spoke candidly about the challenges he'd faced over his career. Although our lived experiences were vastly different, Craig and I connected over the things we had in common. The more we spoke, the more I trusted him with my story and the more he appreciated how one's identity could radically shape their experience at the company.

Although the program was designed to help Craig develop as a leader, it also had a profound impact on me as an individual and employee. Having the CEO take an active interest and curiosity in my life and perspectives made me feel the same sense of validation and empowerment I had felt as a teenager when my teachers started to recognize me. My identity *did* matter, and I could use my voice and skills to make a difference.

At the end of the program, Craig shared what he'd learned from our conversations in a Facebook post. "To make others feel genuinely included, we need to be genuinely curious about them and ask all the questions we don't necessarily feel we need to ask of those most like us," he wrote. "We have to share our own vulnerabilities and create room for the trust that creates real connection." Citing the success of our partnership, the company launched a pilot reverse mentoring program with five mentees from senior leadership and five mentors from diverse backgrounds from other parts of the company. When Virgin Group founder Richard Branson caught wind of the program, he praised it and called me out by name in a LinkedIn post. Shortly after, I began hearing from dozens of people who wanted to learn more and share their own experiences with similar programs. I asked them what had worked well and what hadn't and shared my own insights into how to build a successful mentor-mentee relationship.

Then, in the summer of 2020, the murder of George Floyd and increased violence against Asian people in response to the COVID-19 pandemic sparked outrage and dialogue about the experiences of marginalized groups in predominantly white, patriarchal, Judeo-Christian structures. I realized that the types of conversations I'd had with Craig could potentially help others cut through the chaos and teach us how to reconnect with each other on an individual level, to discover our shared humanity instead of retreating to defensiveness, division, and blame. Obviously, no amount of empathy can effect change unless it's backed up by action, but what did I have to lose by starting the conversation? By encouraging people to be curious about one another, to try to understand each other, so they could make better decisions?

Since that time, I have connected with hundreds of mentors and mentees and have begun working with companies—large and small, across a wide array of industries—to help them set up reverse mentoring schemes. I've heard countless stories from both mentors and mentees about how their perspectives—sometimes even their lives—have changed as a result of the experience.

Take Mark and Amanda. Before meeting each other, Mark hadn't spent a lot of time with people of color. Growing up in the Midwest during the early 2000s, he had heard stories about the plight of people of color and some of the challenges that community faced, but as a white man from a stable middle-class family, he'd never felt the need to concern himself too much with those issues. He knew racism was bad, but he also didn't know what he could possibly do to influence or fix it. And besides, it didn't affect his daily life, and he had other things to worry about.

At the time he met Amanda, Mark was vice president of engineering at a midsize manufacturing company based close to his hometown. He had gone to a local college, was married, and had two children. He traveled frequently—to Europe for work and favored the outdoors for family vacations—but had lived in the same area his entire life. Most of his friends were either from college or from work, and most of them were white with similar backgrounds.

Recently, Mark's company had been acquired by a large firm that was incredibly focused on diversity, equity, and inclusion (DEI). Both their annual and three-year strategic plans included specific sections dedicated to increasing the level of inclusivity within the workplace. As part of that effort, company leadership had mandated that everyone in the organization complete DEI training and that leaders, like Mark, would have to meet certain DEI targets in order to receive their full bonuses. Mark didn't really get it. Shouldn't the right person perform the role, regardless of their gender, ethnicity, sexuality, or any other external factor? As long as everyone was treated with respect and given a fair shot to succeed, did it really matter how diverse the company was?

As part of the integration process following the acquisition, the board of directors requested that the entire leadership team participate in a reverse mentoring program, which would pair senior leaders with more-junior people in the company from different demographic backgrounds. The goal, Mark was told, was to expose the lead decision-makers to perspectives and ideas from people with different lived experiences in an effort to make the company more inclusive and, hopefully, better overall. Mark wasn't keen to participate, but everyone else was doing it and he didn't want to look like a poor sport, so he reluctantly agreed and was paired with Amanda.

At first, Mark saw little difference between him and Amanda beyond the fact that she was of mixed heritage— Native American, Black, and Latinx—and had attended an

Ivy League college. She was born and raised locally, just like Mark, and had had a great career with the company so far. She had been promoted twice in her seven-year tenure and was currently the head of customer experience, three layers below Mark in the organizational chart. She lived locally, had two children, and was married, just like Mark.

"Amanda was great at her job," Mark later observed. "I saw her 'ethnicity' second. Actually, I didn't even 'see' her ethnicity."

But as their conversations deepened, Amanda shared details about her life that gradually revealed some stark differences in their lived experiences. Unlike Mark, who vacationed at least twice per year with his family, Amanda mostly took time off to take care of her children, be-cause—as it is for many married mothers—most childcare duties fell to her. Given that 90 percent of the people in Mark's friendship and work circles were men, Mark had never really considered how these additional responsibil-ities might impact someone's career, even though his own wife had stopped working to become a full-time stay-at-home mom after the birth of their first child. Mark had just assumed that his wife was okay with this arrangement as they'd never really discussed her returning to work and Mark earned enough to support the whole family. Talking to Amanda, Mark began to appreciate how the choice to start a family often impacted mothers more than fathers.

"Amanda never revealed that she felt this held her back in any way and didn't appear resentful of her responsibilities," he said. "However, I wondered if she would be further up the ladder if she didn't have all of this to contend with. I know for sure that I would struggle if it were me—not only doing my day job but doing it exceptionally well as Amanda appears to be doing."

He also learned that, when Amanda was growing up, her parents had chosen to live in a very small house, in which Amanda shared a single room with her three siblings, so they could afford to send their kids to college. Once Amanda got to college, she had to work two jobs in order to afford tuition and other expenses. This meant that she didn't have time for a lot of the extracurricular or social activities that were typical for many of her more well-off peers and, in Mark's case, had been a highlight of his college experience. She started working full-time immediately upon graduation, but most of her extra income went to helping her parents and her siblings who were still in college. When she and her husband finally saved up enough cash to buy a house, her parents moved in with them. Both of her parents still worked—her father as an engineer, her mother as a nurse—but the arrangement made more financial sense. Plus, when they weren't working, her parents could help with the grandkids.

Mark was shocked to learn that a hardworking family like Amanda's could still be so challenged financially, but her experience is actually part of a much larger trend among people and families of color. Due to a variety of factors like differences in opportunities and education, discrimination, a gap in access to financial resources, and relative ability to accumulate (and benefit from) generational wealth, families of color are, on average, far less financially stable than white ones. In 2019 the Federal Reserve survey of consumer finances showed that the median net worth is $188,000 for a white household, $36,000 for a Latinx household, and $24,000 for a Black household.* These are some stark, irrefutable facts.

Mark was also surprised to learn that, despite being promoted twice in her short tenure at the company, Amanda had declined to apply for a third promotion because she thought it was out of her reach. When her boss didn't encourage her, she took it as confirmation that she wasn't ready and watched the job go to a colleague of hers who *had* applied, despite being less qualified and experienced than Amanda. She said:

> I have a feeling my boss has a soft spot for [the man who got the promotion] as they sometimes hang out with each other after work and I have heard them talking about hobbies they have in common. Who has time for hobbies?! I feel really left out when these conversations

*"Why JPMorgan Chase Is Committed to Improving Racial Equity in Banking," *Cold Call* podcast, episode 157, September 21, 2021, https://hbr.org/podcast /2021/09/why-jpmorgan-chase-is-committed-to-improving-racial-equity -in-banking; Neil Bhutta, Andrew C. Chang, Lisa J. Dettling, and Joanne W. Hsu, "Disparities in Wealth by Race and Ethnicity in the 2019 Survey of Consumer Finances," Federal Reserve, September 28, 2020, https://www.federalreserve.gov /econres/notes/feds-notes/disparities-in-wealth-by-race-and-ethnicity-in-the -2019-survey-of-consumer-finances-20200928.htm.

happen, but I just keep my head down and focus on doing an amazing job. I am really disappointed, though,
that, in relation to the promotion, my demonstrable
performance didn't support me in the way that I thought
it should have. I wish I had applied for the promotion,
but on the other hand I just didn't want to be disappointed again.

She'd also recently found out that another colleague—a
man—was paid the same as her despite being more junior.
When she asked human resources about it, they told her
that the "market had changed" since she started and that if
she wanted to be paid market rate, she should "look else-
where." "It didn't really surprise me, but it did disappoint
me," Amanda said. "At the moment I can't move jobs as I
have managed to get the organization of my personal life
down to a fine art. I will have to stick around here for the
foreseeable future."

For nine months, over the course of six sessions, Mark
and Amanda discussed how their lived experiences had
shaped their lives and careers, and Mark began to understand
how being an educated, white, straight, cisgender male in an
environment dominated by other educated, white, straight,
cisgender men had afforded him certain advantages over
Amanda that had nothing to do with their respective talent, knowledge, or skills. He also began to appreciate how
his role as a leader within the company gave him a unique
position to address these inequities. As he and Amanda de-

veloped a closer professional and personal relationship, he began to feel a certain sense of responsibility for her, to use what he'd learned to become a better leader and advocate for people who often don't have a seat at the table.

Mark later became an advocate for Amanda in rooms in which she wasn't present, asking "What about Amanda?" when discussing new projects or having performance conversations with other leaders at the company. He checked in on her regularly, and they developed a mutually beneficial relationship. Amanda was able to share her story with someone who, over time, became more interested in it, while Mark became more conscious of some of the underlying circumstances that could be at play with people on his team specifically. Eight months after his mentoring had started, his team performed a 360-degree feedback survey in which his peers and reports were asked to give honest, constructive feedback on Mark's leadership style. Overall, they reported a noticeable degree of improvement in his level of empathy. Mark had always thought that he was pretty empathetic, but he realized through his experience with Amanda that because he hadn't truly understood the experiences of people from different backgrounds, he didn't fully appreciate what challenges they might be facing on any given day. It's difficult to solve a problem when you don't even know a problem exists. Mark says:

> Before I started on this journey, I believed, based on my experience, that our organization really did practice

meritocracy. That the most capable person would get the promotions and opportunities. That, irrespective of your background, our organization will respect and honor your contributions. I entered into this with little expectation and, to be honest, little curiosity, I suppose an arrogance. At the end of this formal journey, I am more aware of my privilege than I have ever been. I am not ashamed to say that, nor am I in a position where I am shirking away from the responsibilities that are on my shoulders, not only as a leader in the organization but as a more conscious human being. Understanding Amanda's experience has made me more curious than ever, and I am committed to making a difference and raising the awareness of others, too.

ભ્ય૭

In a utopian world, everyone would have a voice that would be heard *and* listened to. Climbing the economic and organizational ladder would reflect the hours worked, effort exerted, and education earned. True meritocracy— in which people attain success, power, and influence based on their talents, knowledge, and performance—would thrive. The school, college, or university you attended; the region or country where you were born; your race, gender identity, disability, sexual orientation, or body shape; how you choose to dress or wear your hair—none of this would matter. The best ideas would win out over the loudest voices, and great employees would be rewarded with great jobs and salaries to match their potential and contributions.

Many organizations say that they aspire to this ideal, but few (if any) have actually achieved it. In fact, research suggests that when companies actively try to promote meritocracy, they often end up favoring dominant demographic groups, like men, over the traditionally marginalized, even when performance is equal.[*]

Who a person is rather than what they do still has a profound effect on what jobs they get, how much influence they hold, and how much money they make. And whether we want to admit it or not, statistics show that, across the globe, certain demographic groups are more likely to succeed than others. In the United States and United Kingdom, women make up just 21 and 18 percent of executive teams, respectively. Globally, women represent just 15 percent.[†] Just five of the London Stock Exchange FTSE 100[‡] and thirty-seven of the US Fortune 500 CEOs[§] are

---

[*] Emilio J. Castilla and Stephen Benard, "The Paradox of Meritocracy in Organizations," *Administrative Science Quarterly* 55, no. 4 (December 2010): 543–576, https://ideas.wharton.upenn.edu/wp-content/uploads/2018/07/Castilla-Benard-2010.pdf.

[†] Sundiatu Dixon-Fyle, Kevin Dolan, Vivian Hunt, and Sara Prince, "Diversity Wins: How Inclusion Matters," McKinsey & Company, May 2020, https://www.mckinsey.com/featured-insights/diversity-and-inclusion/diversity-wins-how-inclusion-matters, 16.

[‡] Barney Cotton, "Discover the Female FTSE 100 CEOs of 2020," *Business Leader*, March 18, 2020, https://www.businessleader.co.uk/discover-the-female-ftse-100-ceos-of-2020/81145/.

[§] Tacy Byham, "Women CEOs' Highest Representation on the Fortune 500 List Still Isn't Enough," *Forbes*, August 3, 2020, https://www.forbes.com/sites/forbescoaches council/2020/08/03/women-ceos-highest-representation-on-the-fortune-500-list-still-isnt-enough/.

women. In the United Kingdom, non-white individuals fill just 4.7 percent (fifty-two) of the 1,099 most powerful roles in the country, despite representing 13 percent of the population.[*] In the United States, just 3.4 percent of Fortune 500 CEOs are from Latinx backgrounds, and a paltry 1 percent are Black, even though those groups represent 18 and 13 percent of the population, respectively.[†] Ethnic diversity is not just a problem in predominantly white countries, either. Globally, just 14 percent of executive teams are composed of people from ethnic minority groups in those regions.[‡]

When organizations don't adequately reflect and represent the communities, customers, and employees they serve, everyone loses. At a systemic level, inequality and lack of representation lead to oppression, violence, harassment, discrimination, and death—a fact most recently highlighted by the work of social justice movements like Black Lives Matter, Me Too, and Stop Asian Hate, just to name a few. It's worth noting, of course, that these are not new movements. But with the world standing still a little more due to the COVID-19 pandemic, we've been forced, as a society, to pay more attention to them than we might have previously.

---

[*] Simon Woolley and Rita Patel, "The Colour of Power 2021," Operation Black Vote, accessed November 2021, https://thecolourofpower.com/.

[†] Daniel Kurt, "Corporate Leadership by Race," Investopedia, July 21, 2021, https://www.investopedia.com/corporate-leadership-by-race-5114494.

[‡] Dixon-Fyle et al., "Diversity Wins."

Though no single diversity, equity, and inclusion policy can right the wrongs of generations of racism, sexism, homophobia, transphobia, and ableism, organizations hold a tremendous amount of power and responsibility to make a difference, particularly in their role as employers. Jobs, after all, create wealth, and wealth creates opportunities. And when people have opportunities, they become empowered. When individuals can use their skills at jobs where they earn a fair wage, are rewarded fairly for their contributions, and feel safe, respected, and supported, it creates a ripple effect. Workers benefit from economic security as well as the confidence and lack of stress that comes from being adequately recognized; organizations benefit from the contributions and energies of a talented, engaged, and diverse workforce; and society benefits from dismantling stereotypes and empowering citizens to lead happy, healthy, and productive lives.

The fact that it's the right thing to do should be enough of a reason for organizations to make diversity a priority, especially because research shows that companies with more diversity perform better than those that lack it. In a two-year study of 200 companies, researchers found that teams representing people of different ages, genders, and geographic locations made better decisions more frequently than those composed mostly of people from similar demographic backgrounds. Inclusive teams performed 60 percent better than the average, and, in fact, the more diverse the team was, the better their performance.[*] Companies with the most diverse leadership teams are more likely to achieve above-average profitability than those with the least amount of diversity. According to a global, multi-year study by McKinsey and Company, companies with the least amount of diversity on their executive teams were 27 percent more likely to *underperform* than any other companies in their data set, and the performance gap between the most and least diverse companies is widening rapidly.[†] In other words, the longer you choose to deprioritize diversity in your organization, the worse off you will be in the future.

When leadership teams are similar and share the same social circles, it is difficult for true independent disagreement to occur because people fear that any overt challenge or dissent may harm their reputations or personal lives. This can create a harmonious workplace (at least on the surface), but it usually leads to disastrous results for the business. Cognitive diversity—which occurs when you bring together people from different backgrounds, demographics, and experiences—fixes this problem by creating an environment in which differing perspectives and opinions are encouraged.

---

[*] Erik Larson, "New Research: Diversity + Inclusion = Better Decision Making at Work," *Forbes*, September 21, 2017, https://www.forbes.com/sites/erik larson/2017/09/21/new-research-diversity-inclusion-better-decision-making-at -work/.

[†] Dixon-Fyle et al., "Diversity Wins."

Many organizations understand the calls for more diversity within their ranks, and have taken at least some steps toward addressing the issue head-on. Nowadays, it's not uncommon for companies to include a statement about their commitment to diversity, equity, and inclusion in their corporate handbooks, on career webpages, and among their core values. Many offer recruitment programs, internships, or networking groups in an effort to support employees from diverse backgrounds. They host events, workshops, and specialized training to help address and reduce biases among employees, and they compose official policies for reporting and punishing discrimination so that such behavior is discouraged. They institute controls in their hiring, interview, and job-placement processes to even the playing field for job candidates and highlight their efforts on their websites to help attract diverse job applicants.

In 2020, in the wake of George Floyd's murder and COVID-19's catastrophic impact on women and people of color, many companies started prioritizing diversity even more than they had in the past. Seemingly overnight, corporate social media feeds overflowed with posts declaring their commitment to solving the problem from the inside out. Human resources teams scrambled to hire diversity consultants and register for implicit bias training. The number of positions with the title of chief diversity officer, director of diversity, or head of diversity increased 68, 75, and 107 percent, respectively, from just five years earlier.* Even before these twin global events, hiring trends showed a dramatic increase in a focus on diversity, with the number of diversity-related job listings increasing 30 percent in the United States, 37 percent worldwide, and a whopping 106 percent in the United Kingdom between 2018 and 2019.†

Unfortunately, despite spending an estimated $8 billion *each year* on diversity, equity, and inclusion initiatives, very few of these efforts end up paying off.‡ A high number of diversity practitioners do not have a long tenure with the same organization, citing "lack of resources, unrealistic expectations and inadequate support from senior executives."§ Meanwhile, implicit bias training, which seeks to acknowledge and correct the hidden prejudices that shape our decisions and interactions, is often ineffective, at best, and, when done poorly, can actually increase the amount of anger, frustration, and division within an

---

* Gerri Mason Hall and Pascale Thorre, "The Rise of Diversity and Inclusion Roles Across Europe and the Middle East," LinkedIn Talent Solutions, accessed November 29, 2021, https://business.linkedin.com/talent-solutions/resources/talent-acquisition/the-rise-of-diversity-and-inclusion.

† Andrew Chamberlain, "Glassdoor's Job & Hiring Trends for 2020," Glassdoor Economic Research, November 12, 2019, https://www.glassdoor.com/research/job-hiring-trends-2020/, 18.

‡ Theresa Agovino, "What Will the Workplace Look Like in 2025?" SHRM, accessed September 7, 2021, https://www.shrm.org/hr-today/news/all-things-work/pages/the-workplace-in-2025.aspx.

§ Chip Cutter and Lauren Weber, "Demand for Chief Diversity Officers Is High. So Is Turnover," *The Wall Street Journal*, July 13, 2020, https://www.wsj.com/articles/demand-for-chief-diversity-officers-is-high-so-is-turnover-11594638000.

organization.* Studies show that many of the things companies do to deter discrimination can often have the opposite of the intended effect, actually *reducing* overall diversity within the organization and creating more tension and friction between groups from different backgrounds.† We see this happen when those in the dominant group(s) (usually white, heterosexual, cisgender men) report feeling less included—even discriminated against—when their organization begins to prioritize DEI, not understanding (as Mark initially didn't) that these changes are not about punishing people from certain groups but about leveling the playing field so that everyone—regardless of race, sexuality, gender, socioeconomic group, or any other demographic factor—has the same opportunities and feels like a valued member of the organization.

SEARCHING FOR A BETTER SOLUTION

Obviously, if we really want to create diverse and inclusive organizations—ones that adequately represent the needs of the people they serve and where the best ideas, people, and efforts are rewarded—we need to revise our approach.

---

* Tiffany L. Green and Nao Hagiwara, "The Problem with Implicit Bias Training," *Scientific American*, August 28, 2020, https://www.scientificamerican.com/article/the-problem-with-implicit-bias-training/.

† Frank Dobbin and Alexandra Kalev, "Why Diversity Programs Fail," *Harvard Business Review*, July–August 2016, 52–60, https://hbr.org/2016/07/why-diversity-programs-fail.

For starters, we need to do more than just pay lip service to the idea. Diversity is not a task that can be checked off a to-do list. Systemic problems require systemic solutions, ones that inform the entire culture of an organization, not the isolated efforts of employee resource groups, human resources, or a few well-meaning individuals (often applying their own discretionary, unpaid efforts on top of full workloads). Trying to retrofit inclusivity onto a fundamentally exclusive organization, regardless of whether that organization's leadership is aware of its prejudices or not, is like trying to decorate a house that has no walls; if you lack a solid foundation, no amount of thoughtful touches can create a functional home.

What we need is an approach that changes the overall culture of an organization. We need one in which every person, especially but not exclusively those in leadership, intrinsically believes that diversity, equity, and inclusion are fundamental for an organization and its people to thrive. To do that, one must change the hearts and minds of those people—the people who create our cultures. If you've ever tried to win an argument, you know this is easier said than done, but it is possible.

People change their minds when presented with evidence that contradicts their current beliefs and opinions, but when it comes to things like race, gender, and identity, there are too many factors at play to rely on statistics alone. Instead, we need to rely on our humanity and empathy— the stories, ideas, feelings, and desires that connect us all beyond our demographics. We do not develop this through a lecture, training, or listening session. The journey to equity and inclusion is a long and hard one. Oftentimes, it requires challenging—or letting others challenge—the beliefs, thoughts, and assumptions that we may have developed as children, things we have accepted as fact, consciously or not, for most of our lives. The journey also requires us to acknowledge our mistakes, our ignorance, and the times we may have been complicit in upholding norms and ideas that harm others. This is extraordinarily difficult to do. No one likes to admit when they've done something to hurt someone else. No one likes to admit when they're wrong. Even obvious bigots often take offense when you refer to them as bigots because they don't like it when people suggest that the worldview that has shaped their choices and behaviors is fundamentally flawed. Going on this journey, committing to the hard road ahead, requires equal parts courage and humility.

Change does not happen with a one-off diversity training or listening session. It does not happen because your organization hires more people of color or promotes more women to leadership positions. It does not happen because of an anti-discrimination policy codified by lawyers and printed in the employee handbook. It happens when people—real people with all their flaws and attributes—change from the inside out. If we want to promote this kind of change, we need a tool that promotes dialogue, connection, empathy, and vulnerability between multiple parties and that allows people from disparate backgrounds to truly engage with and understand one another. Enter reverse mentoring.

WHAT IS REVERSE MENTORING?

Think back to the story that opened this chapter. When Mark first met Amanda, he was unaware that there was a problem with diversity and inclusion at his company. He didn't consider himself someone with special advantages or privileges. He had gone to school and worked his way up the corporate ladder through consistent effort and skill, and the fact that Amanda had also been promoted several times showed that she was well on her way to doing the same. But as he got to know her better, he began to appreciate that, even though on paper they may have had the same opportunities, in practice Amanda had to work harder to reach her goals because of her status as a working mother and as a person from a relatively less-well-off economic bracket, not to mention a woman from a multi-ethnic, non-white background. Mark had access to the same statistics everyone else has; he knew that BIPOC people and women were subject to certain stereotypes and discrimination, and that they represented fewer people in leadership positions across various industries. But it was his conversations with Amanda that helped humanize the issue and the impact identity has on people's ability to get ahead in the world.

Mark and Amanda may have eventually met through their roles in the office, but it's unlikely that they would have had the types of conversations they had in those circumstances. Instead, they were brought together as part of their company's reverse mentoring program, which was part of their larger DEI strategy. Although the concept of mentoring has existed for generations, and many organizations have adopted some type of formal mentoring program for employees, reverse mentoring is a relatively new phenomenon.

The concept is exactly what it sounds like—a mentoring arrangement in which the standard roles of mentor and mentee are reversed. Unlike a traditional mentoring relationship in which a more experienced and/or more senior individual shares advice and information with a less experienced (usually younger) colleague, reverse mentoring tasks less tenured (often younger) employees with sharing their perspectives, skills, and insights with those who have more decision-making power. Essentially, the person who would normally be the novice becomes the master. Reverse mentoring acknowledges that, though they may lack the experience and institutional or industry knowledge of those higher up the chain of command, less-senior employees often have a wealth of experiences—personal and professional—that could help leaders make better decisions, thus, in turn, allowing the company to remain more competitive.

First popularized by Jack Welch, the hugely influential CEO of General Electric, in 1999, reverse mentoring has typically been used by organizations looking to bridge generational gaps. Welch, observing the rise of the Internet at the dawn of the twenty-first century and business's increasing dependence on emerging technologies, realized that his company would suffer a huge disadvantage if the people in charge of determining company policy and strategy (many of whom had come of age during a time when the World Wide Web was basically science fiction) didn't understand the tools on which their industry was coming to rely. Welch asked 500 of his top managers to find a young employee to teach them about the Internet, and the success of that experiment spurred interest in the concept across the corporate world. Since then, several other organizations, including powerhouses like Cisco, Target, PricewaterhouseCoopers, and Hewlett Packard, have developed similar programs with similar results. Companies that have instituted comprehensive reverse mentoring programs report reduced turnover, improved skills transfer, and better insight into problems that they previously did not understand or know existed.[*] Reverse mentoring has been shown to boost retention and keep people more engaged so they are less likely to leave.[†] This last point is especially key when considering

[*] Jason Wingard, "Reverse Mentoring: 3 Proven Outcomes Driving Change," *Forbes*, August 8, 2018, https://www.forbes.com/sites/jasonwingard/2018/08/08/reverse-mentoring-3-proven-outcomes-driving-change/.

[†] Laura Earle, "How to Set Up a Reverse Mentoring Program in 10 Steps," *Cisco Blogs*, February 19, 2014, https://blogs.cisco.com/diversity/how-to-set-up-a-reverse-mentoring-program-in-10-steps.

that millennials, who will represent the largest segment (44 percent) of the workforce by 2025 and tend to change jobs more frequently than their older counterparts, cite mentoring support as the most important factor determining their decision to stay with a company.[*]

The success of reverse mentoring in terms of technical experience has led some organizations to expand the program to address other types of diversity, particularly when it comes to underrepresented groups. Although the body of research into the effectiveness of these initiatives is still relatively small, there is a lot of early and qualitative data showing that, when executed intentionally and consistently alongside a robust existing DEI program, reverse mentoring may be one of the most effective tools available to combat bias, stereotypes, and discrimination, with an overall goal to increase inclusivity and equity.

Reverse mentoring works by promoting empathy and narrowing the gap between perceived differences in individuals. Human beings tend to affiliate themselves with people from the same social, demographic, and geographic circles as them—a phenomenon known as affinity bias. White people tend to associate with other white people. Immigrants tend to affiliate with other immigrants from the same geographic or ethnographic regions. College-educated people tend to associate with

---

[*] Catrin Hechl, "Affective Commitment to Organizations: A Comparative Study of Reverse Mentoring Versus Traditional Mentoring Among Millennials," *Binus Business Review* 8, no. 2 (August 2017): 157–165.

other college-educated people. Political conservatives tend to associate with political conservatives. And so on. Most of us don't do this intentionally—it's the way we're wired, a holdover from ancient days when different people often represented threats to ourselves and our families. But in our modern world, where our communities are growing less homogenous by the minute, our affinity biases can prevent us from fully integrating and cooperating with those around us.

When we choose to surround ourselves with people who are different—who look different, believe different things, and have experienced different things—we actively dismantle this bias by becoming more attuned to their lived experience instead of just our own.

It's one thing to read an article about police brutality. It's another to hear a Black colleague—someone you work side-by-side with every day—talk about his experience of being threatened or beaten by a police officer at a routine traffic stop.

It's one thing to read statistics about how difficult it is for working mothers to get ahead in their careers. It's another to see the dark circles under a female colleague's eyes after staying up all night nursing her newborn.

It's one thing to hear about the persecution and violence that queer, trans, and nonbinary people experience in certain parts of the world. It's another to learn about the extra precautions your gay coworker has to take when they travel abroad for work.

Reverse mentoring helps to break down barriers and promote empathy and understanding of diverse groups by creating a safe, structured, intentional, and intimate space for people to share stories and information they might not otherwise hear. Similar to traditional mentoring, it seeks to transfer knowledge and best practices through an ongoing, one-on-one relationship. When done well, the process benefits both parties equally. The mentee learns new perspectives and gains insights into a group to which they previously didn't have access and can use that knowledge to inform their decisions and strategies going forward. The mentor benefits from the opportunity to share their ideas and opinions directly with a senior leader or peer and by having the chance to make a positive impact on the organization. By extension, the organization benefits from having a more knowledgeable leadership team who are better equipped to make decisions and a workforce of more-junior employees who feel respected and valued.

As with all diversity programs, of course, the potential for error is high. If a company has a history of failed DEI initiatives or a culture that excludes or marginalizes certain groups, a reverse mentoring program is unlikely to work unless a few foundational elements are put into place first. In this book, I will draw on my experience studying and implementing reverse mentoring programs to walk you through what an effective reverse mentoring program looks like—and what pitfalls to avoid.

In the chapters that follow, I will lay out a step-by-step process for setting up a reverse mentoring program and the best practices to keep in mind for the highest chance of success. I'll start by describing the organizational prerequisites you need to have in place before a reverse mentoring program can succeed. I'll then move on to dedicate a chapter to each of the three main roles for the program: human resources, the mentor, and the mentee. These chapters will guide you through how to approach your role as well as tips for handling difficult situations, disagreements, or disappointments. You'll then learn how to run each meeting—with special attention on the first session—followed by a primer on how to share the insights gleaned within these meetings with the rest of the organization and turn them into action so that, over time, they are woven into the fabric of the culture.

By using our own stories to bring more humanity into our organizations, reverse mentoring allows us to see one another and ourselves in a radically new light. Only when we look at the world differently can we decide to make change—change that, in this case, is long overdue and sorely needed. Let's begin.

CHAPTER TWO

A FOUNDATION OF TRUST

Imagine that your boss comes to you one day and announces that your company has decided to adopt a brand-new piece of cutting-edge technology that will radically transform the way you work. After listening to employees complain about inefficient workflows, poor communication between teams, and an inability to stay organized and on budget, a group of high-level managers and executives got together to find a solution. When they started hearing buzz about this new product and how it had helped other organizations, including a few of your competitors, they unanimously decided to invest hundreds of thousands of dollars in the highest-level enterprise version so every single employee could start using it right away.

At first, you're thrilled. Your company has been experiencing a lot of growing pains lately, and you and your teammates have been struggling to meet deadlines and stay on budget. You take it as a good sign that management is finally recognizing this issue and has decided to make fixing it a priority.

There's just one problem: despite the huge amount of money spent on the product, the company doesn't invest any time or resources into training the rest of you on how to use it. They tell you that it's intuitive, that it will all make sense once everyone adopts it and integrates it into their daily life.

The tool certainly looks cool and does appear to have a lot of features that, in theory at least, would make your life easier. But, as you start to work with it, you find it's actually making your life harder. It takes you twice as long to log a task as it does to complete the task, and no one seems to know how to share information on the platform so you end up wasting more precious time sending emails or holding meetings to clear up confusion. Within just a few weeks, you and your colleagues abandon the tool. Things are just as inefficient as before, if not more so. The company has lost tons of money, not to mention time, and employees are now angry that their concerns weren't properly addressed. The worst part? The tool probably could have fixed most of your problems—if people had been trained on how to use it.

In many ways reverse mentoring is like this type of cutting-edge technology. When people use it correctly, it can literally change lives and reshape the entire culture of an organization. It can improve communication, increase engagement, and make the company stronger as a whole over time. But when it's done poorly, when those who participate are not given the tools and knowledge to use it properly, it not only is a waste of time and energy, but it can end up doing more harm than good.

Diversity, equity, and inclusion initiatives are notoriously difficult to embed because they require participants to be honest and open about some of the hardest, most personal things in their lives. People from marginalized groups don't want to relive the trauma of their experiences or open themselves up to more discrimination or bias (whether explicit or implicit). They don't want to draw attention to what makes them different because they fear that it will overshadow the other qualities that define them. They worry about being perceived negatively or not being taken seriously. For example:

- Will I be labeled a complainer?
- Will admitting I have to work twice as hard mean I will be incorrectly considered incapable?
- With whom will my stories be shared outside of the conversation?
- What if my feelings are minimized?

Reverse mentoring is particularly difficult to implement because it requires people to discuss the most personal (sometimes painful) details of their lives in an intimate, one-on-one setting while simultaneously reversing the roles of authority that typically exist within an organization. Only recently have organizations been encouraging their employees to "show up as their whole selves" to work, and there are still a lot of stereotypes around what is considered "professional" or appropriate to discuss with colleagues. Asking people to talk about their life experiences with someone they probably don't know very well and who probably holds more authority than them in the organization is asking those individuals to put themselves in an inherently uncomfortable, potentially threatening position.

And it's not just a challenge for mentors. In a reverse mentoring situation, the person used to holding the role of teacher assumes the role of student. This requires a certain amount of humility and vulnerability that—no matter how well placed their intentions—they may struggle to accept. Individuals from more dominant demographic backgrounds often don't want to admit their ignorance, privilege, or complicity within an existing system of oppression. They may not want to think of themselves as biased and may get defensive if they feel that they're being accused as such.

- If they're used to being listened to, they may have trouble listening.
- If they're used to being the smartest person in the room, they may have trouble admitting their ignorance about a specific topic.

- If they believe that they ascended to their position through hard work, intelligence, and sound judgment alone, they may not want to admit that their gender, sexuality, race, economic status, or any other quality outside their control had anything to do with their success.

Organizations must recognize that when mentors and mentees agree to participate in a reverse mentoring program, they are entrusting their mental and emotional health to the organization in the hopes that their efforts will create positive change. Everyone, even the most open-minded and growth-oriented among us, has an ego. And though it's impossible to control the actions and emotions of others, it is important that companies put the necessary systems and controls in place to ensure that things can continue to run smoothly even if conflict arises.

The reason that so many DEI initiatives fail is not because they are inherently useless or ineffective; it's because they're not deployed in an environment designed to make them successful. Such an environment requires trust. Trust exists within an organization when employees believe that their leaders are telling them the truth, when they believe that they are treated with respect, and when they believe that the dynamics of the workplace are fundamentally fair.*

---

* *The Business Case for a High-Trust Culture*, Great Place to Work, 2016, https://www.greatplacetowork.ca/images/reports/Business_Case_for_High_Trust_Culture.pdf, 3.

When trust does not exist, employees are more likely to experience stress, burnout, illness, disengagement, and lack of energy, all of which make it less likely that they'll want to participate in a program. A program that not only asks them to volunteer additional time and energy, but requires vulnerability, candor, debate, and empathy, cannot work without trust.*

Before you launch a reverse mentoring program, you need to audit the level of trust within your organization and ensure that certain measures are in place to protect and/or build that trust and improve it going forward. The rest of this chapter will provide a roadmap for achieving this, but the specifics of your program will depend on your goals as an organization and the level of trust that currently exists. If you already have a strong DEI program in place and have demonstrated authentic commitment through consistent, thoughtful actions that diversity, equity, and inclusion are a priority, then you probably already have the foundation for a successful reverse mentoring program. Still, it's worth taking the time to assess what you hope to get out of the program and how it fits within your overall goals so you can communicate that to participants and any other stakeholders in the organization. If your DEI program is in its infancy and/or you've made mistakes in the past that have undermined the level of trust in your organization, then it may take a while—possibly years—to create

---

* Paul J. Zak, "The Neuroscience of Trust," *Harvard Business Review*, January–February 2017, 84–90, https://hbr.org/2017/01/the-neuroscience-of-trust.

the level of safety you need for reverse mentoring to work. Don't let that discourage you. If you are truly committed to improving diversity, equity, and inclusion, these steps are necessary and worth the time and energy that it takes to do them right.

DIVERSITY FROM THE TOP DOWN

Before we get started, it's important to make one thing clear: none of these steps will work if your company is not ready to make diversity, equity, and inclusion a priority at the highest level of management. For these programs to be successful, they need to be given the same level of attention and resources as any other strategic initiative that the company is pursuing. Too often, companies are so focused on hitting next quarter's revenue targets that they treat DEI as an extracurricular activity—something nice to work on in their spare time, but easy to forget about if there are more "pressing" things on their minds. But, as we've acknowledged, an inclusive culture is not a "nice-to-have"; it's essential for the overall, long-term health of the organization and its people.

Ideally, you should have someone in place whose main goal is to serve as the custodian of DEI within the organization. Though we know that DEI is everyone's job, having one person or team responsible for overseeing it will ensure that it remains a priority in larger conversations about strategy, culture, and goals. At larger companies, this could be a chief diversity officer or someone with a similar title. At smaller ones, the responsibility would be part of the overall business strategy held centrally within human resources. Regardless, this person or team's performance should be measured on their ability to set and meet DEI goals, and they should be given the same level of authority as every other team within the organization. They should be included in all leadership, strategy, and planning conversations and have a slot on every meeting agenda. DEI metrics should be included in all quarterly or annual surveys and reviews, and the head of the DEI program should have the same opportunities to communicate with leadership, board members, managers, and employees as any other executive.

Doing this not only ensures that DEI stays top of mind, but it also signals that those in charge of steering the company's direction consider diversity, equity, and inclusion to be more than just buzzwords or branding. People trust leaders who are authentic, vulnerable, and humble, who lead by example, who acknowledge their shortcomings, and who commit—truly commit—to doing better. You cannot ask a mid-level manager to care about something that the CEO doesn't care about. You cannot ask a junior employee to participate in a reverse mentoring program— and potentially risk their reputation, mental health, or career prospects—if they don't believe that those in charge care about what they have to say. Giving diversity the same respect as sales, marketing, research and development, or any other traditionally profit-centric division demonstrates that leadership considers it a priority—and that everyone else should, too.

THE FOUR-A AUDIT

Once you identify the person or people in charge of leading your diversity, equity, and inclusion initiatives, you can begin the process of laying the foundation for a successful reverse mentoring program. This should happen in four broad stages:

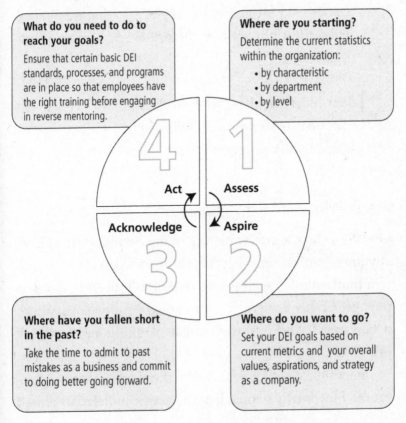

What do you need to do to reach your goals?

Ensure that certain basic DEI standards, processes, and programs are in place so that employees have the right training before engaging in reverse mentoring.

Where are you starting?

Determine the current statistics within the organization:
- by characteristic
- by department
- by level

4 Act

1 Assess

3 Acknowledge

2 Aspire

Where have you fallen short in the past?

Take the time to admit to past mistakes as a business and commit to doing better going forward.

Where do you want to go?

Set your DEI goals based on current metrics and your overall values, aspirations, and strategy as a company.

1. **Assess:** Measure the current levels of diversity, equity, inclusion, *and trust* within your organization by gathering data and feedback directly from employees.
2. **Aspire:** Set your DEI goals based on current metrics and your overall values, aspirations, and strategy as a company.
3. **Acknowledge:** Take the time to admit to past mistakes as a business and commit to doing better going forward.
4. **Act:** Ensure that certain basic DEI standards, processes, and programs are in place so that employees have the right training before engaging in reverse mentoring.

Taken together, these four steps will allow you to set up the foundation for a solid DEI strategy, within which a reverse mentoring program is most likely to thrive.

Assess: Where Are You Starting?

Getting a clear, accurate picture of the current state of DEI at your organization is key. If you don't already have a system in place for tracking DEI data, you'll need to develop one, preferably as part of your annual employee survey so it becomes baked into the regular planning and feedback process.

Start by collecting data on the diversity of your organization. How many people from a specific underrepresented group do you employ? How many minorities do you have in leadership positions? How representative is your marketing team compared to your internal population and your clients? How does representation change in your corporate headquarters versus your satellite offices or on the front lines?

Diversity metrics highlight the extent to which different groups are represented within the organization, but diversity does not guarantee inclusion. In an inclusive environment, people from disparate backgrounds feel like they are treated equitably, respectfully, and as valued members of the team. In fact, it is extremely common for diverse organizations to struggle with inclusivity. One study found that, overall, 52 percent of employees report positive feelings about diversity within their organization, while only 29 percent report the same feelings about inclusion.* Therefore, when assessing the current state of your organization, you want to make sure that you're looking at the right data.

Gather data on as many demographic areas as you can. These include race, ethnicity, gender identity, age, religion, sexual orientation, and disability, but there are many other areas you can measure. See the following section for a more exhaustive list. You will likely already have some of this data from previous surveys, job applications, onboarding forms, or insurance enrollment forms. The rest

---

* Dixon-Fyle et al., "Diversity Wins," 34.

you will need to ask for while respecting your employees' right to privacy. Ideally, you would be able to collect this information on each employee so you could better track their specific journey within the organization, but if that's not possible, you can ask for employees to share it anonymously to at least get an overall picture of diversity at the organization. Hopefully, as you work to build trust and communicate why the data is important, more people will feel comfortable disclosing their information and you can build a more robust dataset over time.

≫ THE DIFFERENT TYPES OF DIVERSITY

For all of the areas listed, we recommend (if legally permissible) gathering the information so the organization is able to identify members of various groups and track their careers within the company. This will allow you to assess any patterns that may require corrective action: for example, if women take longer to be promoted than men or people of color stay with the company half as long as white employees.

- Race (defined by Merriam-Webster as "any one of the groups that humans are often divided into based on physical traits regarded as common among people of shared ancestry")
- Ethnicity (Ethnicity is more frequently chosen by the individual. And, because it encompasses everything from language to nationality, culture, and religion, it can enable people to take on several identities. Someone might choose to identify themselves as Asian American,

British Somali, or an Ashkenazi Jew, for instance, drawing on different aspects of their ascribed racial identity,
culture, ancestry, and religion.)

- Sexual orientation
- Gender identity
- Age (We are entering into an era where there will con-
  sistently be up to five generations within the workforce.
  Understanding the majority and minority groups that
  exist will be vital.)
- Religious affiliation
- Disability or chronic illness
- Neurodiversity
- Veteran status (Veterans who have served in the armed
  forces sometimes find it difficult to readjust to civilian
  life, therefore it is important to think about this group
  and commit to the relevant adjustments to ensure that
  they are able to bring their full selves to a supportive
  work environment.)
- Socioeconomic status
- Education level (What is the level of education for the
  majority of the organization? If the majority is the same,
  is there a risk that the organization may suffer from
  "groupthink"? If so, what opportunities and risks could
  you be missing?)
- Parental status
- Immigration or citizenship status
- Incarceration history

If you are able to track the information by individual,
you'll want to break it down to assess diversity in different

areas of the company. Here are a few questions to ask of the data:

- Are there imbalances within the organization—with some teams, locations, or levels looking radically different from others?
- Do people from certain demographic groups tend to stay at the company longer than others?
- Which groups get promoted more quickly?
- Which groups are most engaged?
- Which groups are most represented at the leadership level?
- Are certain people paid more than others for the same work?
- If you have data from previous years, do you notice areas that have become more or less diverse? What might have happened to have caused this?

The more granular you can be, the more you'll be able to spot patterns and gaps and monitor which initiatives are working—and which aren't. What you find may surprise you. For example, in a study of organizations that had won awards for their gender equality interventions, researchers found that the most decorated companies—those who had received awards for their efforts to improve gender equity—often had the highest pay gaps between genders. In fact, 82 percent of award winners actually had a gender-pay gap that was higher than the United Kingdom's national average.* This goes to show that good intentions do not always yield good results.

These numbers help tell a story, but they're only part of the narrative. Companies tend to prefer hard data because they provide information without emotion—numbers don't lie. But numbers also don't account for the full employee experience, nor do they help you measure the level of trust that exists. For that, you'll need to refer to your employee engagement surveys or any other data that measures how your employees perceive the organization. These can include specific diversity surveys, feedback on other DEI programs, or job review websites such as Glassdoor. For your employee survey, pay specific attention to the questions that address happiness and belonging. These include Likert-scale statements such as the following:

- I find that my values and the organization's values are similar.
- I feel like I belong in this company.
- I plan to still be at this company in two years.
- I see a clear connection between the company's mission and my individual job.
- I can be my authentic self at work.
- I believe in the direction in which the company is going.

---

* Stephen Frost and Raafi-Karim Alidina, *Building an Inclusive Organization: Leveraging the Power of a Diverse Workforce* (London: Kogan Page, 2019), 50.

- I believe that my manager understands me as an individual.
- My individual needs are met by my manager.
- I would recommend this organization as a place to work.
- I am proud to be an employee at my company.
- My manager sets clear expectations for my performance.
- I can see myself growing and developing my career in this company.
- This organization really inspires the very best in me when it comes to job performance.

Aspire: Where Do You Want to Go?

Once you've assessed your data and developed a clear sense of where you are, you can figure out where you want to go. When planning a DEI goal, follow the same process as you would when planning any other goal for the company and involve the same people, not just those on the diversity team, so you can ensure buy-in and accountability.

As with any goal, what might be right for another organization may not be right for yours, and you want to aspire to something that you can realistically achieve. Too small of a goal will signal that you're not serious about change. If the goal is too ambitious, this will inevitably raise stress levels for colleagues, leading to frustration, discouragement, resentment, or disengagement. You wouldn't register for your first Ironman Triathlon the week after starting a new exercise program. Don't set yourself up to fail.

To figure out the areas on which to focus, start by considering DEI through the lens of your other goals and values. My employer, Virgin Atlantic, had set a goal of being the world's most-loved airline. In order to do that, they determined that they'd need to be the most inclusive airline because they serve such diverse destinations around the world and knew their customers would feel more inclined to fly with someone who made them feel welcomed.

Consider not just your industry benchmarks but also the diversity of the communities in which you operate and the customers you serve. Up to half of customers from minority groups say that their needs are often unmet by companies, and 47 percent say that their demographic groups are not accurately portrayed in advertising.* When diversity is just branding, people see right through it. Building an inclusive culture from the inside out will help you better serve the people you're trying to reach.

Having a big-picture goal in place will allow you to further analyze your data and develop smaller, more specific goals. For example:

---

* Juliet Bourke and Bernadette Dillon, "The Diversity and Inclusion Revolution: Eight Powerful Truths," *Deloitte Review*, Issue 22, January 22, 2018, https://www2 .deloitte.com/us/en/insights/deloitte-review/issue-22/diversity-and-inclusion-at -work-eight-powerful-truths.html, 92.

- Where are the biggest gaps?
- Is one division lagging behind the rest?
- Do women make up half of overall employees but only 10 percent of executives?
- Are ethnic minorities well represented in your satellite offices but not corporate headquarters?
- Do you cater to a large number of Latinx customers, but your marketing team is exclusively white?
- Where is your representation of disability, sexual orientation, and gender identity?
- How are all religious holidays accommodated?

I once worked with a retailer that had offices and stores all over Europe. However, after assessing their diversity, they found that, despite the fact that several stores were located in neighborhoods with large BIPOC populations, the vast majority of their frontline staff were white or biracial (partially white). Diversity had long been a stated goal of their brand, and they hoped to appeal to people of all backgrounds. But how could they do that if the staff responsible for selling their items didn't reflect the communities they served? They set a goal of having at least 30 percent of their staff in those areas be BIPOC, with specific demographics varying based on the makeup of specific neighborhoods.

This brings us comfortably to addressing another topic of debate: diversity goals.

Some companies push back on the idea of setting specific diversity goals because it feels like they're simply trying to fill a quota. This is a valid concern because tokenism is real and doesn't benefit anyone. Tokenism occurs when companies try to appear diverse by doing performative actions, such as hiring a certain number of individuals from an underrepresented group or highlighting specific individuals for their identity or background rather than their contributions or talents. We see this when someone is described as a "woman in tech" or a "Black founder" or an "LGBTQ leader" or when we expect people with certain backgrounds to act as the de facto spokesperson for that group. This puts a lot of weight on their shoulders and highlights the need for more steps toward inclusion and belonging than diversity.

Diversity without inclusion cannot combat systemic bias or prejudice and usually leaves people feeling used and resentful while perpetuating the myth that minorities can't get ahead on their own merits. That said, it is important to set specific goals, even if they're stretches at first, because they give you a baseline from which to measure progress. We'll discuss more about how to encourage inclusion and avoid tokenism later in the chapter.

Acknowledge: Where Have You Fallen Short in the Past?

For a reverse mentoring program—or any meaningful conversations about identity—to work, you need people to be comfortable feeling vulnerable. Traditionally marginalized groups need to feel okay being vulnerable about their

struggles and difficult experiences, and traditionally dominant groups need to feel okay being vulnerable about their
ignorance and mistakes. The best way to encourage vulnerability is to *show* vulnerability, and that starts with own-
ing up to any mistakes you may have made, promises you
may have broken, naivete you previously had, or actions
you may have failed to take because you thought that they
would be too controversial. This is not easy to do, especially if you've realized some personal bias or are trying to
overcome a toxic workplace culture or problematic leadership. But if you want people to trust you, you can't deny
reality, get defensive, or try to pass the buck. You must own
the mistake, rectify it, and vow to do better going forward.

If there's currently a relatively high level of trust, you
can do this step after you've set your new DEI goals. Use
the opportunity to acknowledge where the gaps are and
what you plan to do to improve, and to announce commitments planned to get there. Chances are, if you're in this
position, you've been doing fairly well with your initiatives thus far and probably already have a system in place
for communicating this sort of progress. Regardless, it's
worthwhile to occasionally pause to make sure that you're
holding yourself accountable and taking the opportunity
to be transparent.

If you've received a lot of complaints or critical feedback about your DEI initiatives or are recovering from an
incident that severely undermined trust, this step becomes
a lot more challenging and a lot more vital. Though it's im-

portant to acknowledge the situation quickly so that people know you're paying attention, words alone, no matter how sincere or well crafted, are never going to suffice. Come up with an action plan to address the situation going forward and commit to sending out regular communications updating people on progress and feedback throughout. In fact, the more information you can share (while protecting people's privacy), the better. In order to integrate fully within the organization and culture, a successful approach to diversity, equity, and inclusion communications has been to *include* it in the regular drumbeat of activities. This constant flow of information integrated with regular business communications helps to normalize the information shared and encourage more consistent conversations.

Act: What Do You Need to Do to Reach Your Goals?

Now that you have clear goals in mind, you can start putting programs and processes in place to achieve them. Remember, your objective is not to fill a quota but to create an inclusive environment that encourages diversity by removing bias and barriers.

The most important thing you need to have in place before you can introduce reverse mentoring is an education and training program that will get employees on the same page when it comes to information, standards of behavior, and company policies. The second is a process for communicating data, goals, feedback, progress, and new initiatives so DEI stays top of mind and people are kept in the loop. Both of these will also help increase trust in the organization because they will indicate a commitment to improving DEI.

It's also worth taking stock of the current recruitment, hiring, and promotion protocols you have in place to ensure that they are aligned with your overall DEI strategy. Though it's not imperative to have all of this in place before you start reverse mentoring, it will help make reverse mentoring more effective and could potentially help increase diversity at your organization with some relatively simple steps. If you need assistance, check out some of the many books, trainings, and online resources available on these topics.

Education and Training

Though there's plenty of evidence that diversity training and education can be ineffective when done in a vacuum, they are essential to building an inclusive culture. People come to an organization with different lived experiences and worldly knowledge. An ongoing education and training program allows you to get everyone on the same page while simultaneously establishing a standard of behavior to which you can hold everyone going forward. I recommend starting with three types of training:

1. **Unconscious bias training:** Foundational, basic training popularized even more in the wake of the

Black Lives Matter movement, this type of training seeks to teach people how our society, experiences, and institutions have trained us to discriminate against and make assumptions about certain groups, often without realizing it. By becoming aware of our unconscious biases, we can put processes into place that help to eliminate them. This will just scratch the surface of the work that the organization needs to do in order to become truly inclusive, but it is nonetheless important to provide this shared framework of understanding.

2. **Microaggression training:** A microaggression is a casual behavior or interaction that belies discrimination—intentional or not—against a traditionally marginalized group. These include things like asking an Asian American where they're from even though they speak perfect English and have no accent or asking a Black person if you can touch their hair. In many cases, people perform microaggressions without intending to be offensive or discriminatory, but good intentions do not excuse bad behavior. By teaching people about microaggressions and why they're hurtful, you can help avoid them. Here are some common microaggressions, which on the surface could seem harmless or even complimentary:

» You're so articulate!
» You're transgender? Wow, you don't look like it at all.

» Oh, you're gay? You should meet my friend Ann. She's gay, too!
» My [female] boss is crazy.
» Where are you actually from?
» The way you've overcome your disability is so inspiring.
» Your name is so hard to pronounce.
» I think you're in the wrong room. This is the [topic] meeting.
» Are you an intern? You look so young!
» Is that your real hair?

3. **Bullying and harassment training:** Such training should not only focus on the most commonly recognized forms of bullying and harassment but also look across the fair treatment of all individuals, ensuring that no bias affects the way they are treated.

If your DEI program is relatively new and/or you've never done these trainings before, I recommend working with an external consultant to either run the trainings or train the DEI team on how to run them effectively. This ensures not only that the training is done correctly but also that employees get all their questions answered by a neutral third party.

Ideally, you should require all employees to take these trainings once a year as part of your annual code of conduct or ethics refresher course, and you should refer back to the trainings when dealing with someone who has been accused of discriminatory behavior. Many companies already use these trainings to protect themselves from lawsuits, but when baked into the culture of the company, and when people are held accountable for following them, they can become a powerful tool toward increasing empathy, awareness, trust, and inclusion. Remember, this is just the basic foundation, a benchmark for organizations to work and build from. The trainings themselves will not create change in the organization; what will is using the teachings from the trainings to change the conversations and actions going on around the organization. Most important is to always enforce such policies by following through on disciplinary or corrective action when someone violates them.

In addition to these standard trainings, it's worth setting up an ongoing education program to address subjects that affect your workplace or are getting attention in the media. For example, after the COVID-19 pandemic hit and conspiracy theories circulated that the virus had been manufactured in China, anti-Asian hate crimes spiked by 169 percent in cities across the United States.[*] As a result, many employees of Asian descent began pointing out the ways in which

---

[*] Kimmy Yam, "New Report Finds 169 Percent Surge in Anti-Asian Hate Crimes During the First Quarter," NBC News, April 28, 2021, https://www.nbcnews.com/news/asian-america/new-report-finds-169-percent-surge-anti-asian-hate-crimes-n1265756.

discrimination affects them at work, forcing employers to confront this reality, perhaps for the first time.* In the past few years, there has been an increase in corporate education around topics such as mental health, menopause, addiction, dyslexia, and other factors that could affect a person's work life. You can also tie these trainings to specific "awareness days" (or weeks, or months), of which there are dozens.† Make these educational programs recurring, regular, intentional, and highly encouraged. One company I worked with hosted a webinar in honor of National Trans Awareness Day in an effort to educate employees about the challenges trans individuals face at work and also in life. One employee I later interviewed disclosed that, not long before this webinar, his transgender son had started the process of transitioning, and my interviewee was finding it particularly difficult to process. The workplace webinar was the first "outside" support he had sought, and this then encouraged him to pursue some further support, leading to a greater level of understanding and empathy for his son. Subsequently, he became more comfortable speaking about his journey of understanding, sharing the emotions and challenges he went through in getting to a place of acceptance.

---

* Christopher S. Tang, "Why Successful Asian Americans Are Penalized at the Workplace," *Los Angeles Times*, May 6, 2021, https://www.latimes.com/opinion/story/2021-05-06/asian-bias-discrimination-corporate-culture-glass-ceiling.

† See the Awareness Days event calendar at https://www.awarenessdays.com/awareness-days-calendar/.

Communication

In order to build trust, it's not enough to implement a strategy; you need to track and share your progress regularly with all stakeholders in the organization. Make sure that diversity is always on the agenda at any leadership meetings and that those tasked with implementing DEI programs are held responsible for their progress. Develop a diversity scorecard to measure areas like recruitment, retention, and promotion across different departments and geographies, and rank them against one another so people can see what's working and what's not. The very act of forcing people to report their progress will make them more likely to commit to the process. In addition, if we take this one step further and link diversity performance to remuneration, then it will also increase the level of commitment. No one likes to be called out publicly for not completing the assignment or, furthermore, to have their income impacted.

Set DEI goals alongside any other financial or strategic goals for the year and report on your progress on the same schedule as other initiatives. Add it to the agenda for board meetings, and include a diversity section in your annual report. Ideally, you should be sharing your results with the executive team once every quarter. If you do so more frequently, you won't have enough time to get fresh data between meetings; if you do so less frequently, you don't give yourself the opportunity to course-correct if a new initiative isn't working.

No organization is perfect, and as long as you're actively building trust within the organization—and monitoring your progress—you will reach a point where you're ready to start a reverse mentoring relationship. In an effort to help gauge your progress, routinely check in with yourself to answer the following questions:

- How much do people trust your organization? You can assess this by adding questions to employee surveys such as these:
    » Do you trust the leaders to make decisions with your best interests at heart?
    » Do you think that the organization communicates transparently?
    » Are you confident that the organization managed the employee and business needs well during [time range]?

- Do people feel like they belong? What is the level of engagement and belonging within the business?
- Are all on board? Are your leaders on board with the journey? If not, then pause and invest in education to ensure that they all have the same level of basic understanding.
- How are you performing across the Four-A audit categories?

If trust is low (below "agree" on the five-part Likert scale), then consider pausing your reverse mentoring program while you work on building trust, or perhaps consider launching your program with a group where trust is high. The same applies for sense of belonging.

CHAPTER THREE

THE ROLE OF HUMAN RESOURCES

As the department responsible for overseeing DEI efforts and managing employee relations, human resources (HR) should be in charge of setting up and running a reverse mentoring program. There are two main things HR needs to do in this role. The first is to create a system that ensures that the program has the highest chance of helping the company accomplish its overall DEI goals. Second, they must ensure the psychological safety of participants. Without these responsibilities in mind, a program will, at best, be a waste of time and, at worst, could undermine existing DEI initiatives as well as trust in the company itself.

The rest of this chapter will walk HR personnel through how to set up a reverse mentoring program for maximum impact.

WHY PSYCHOLOGICAL SAFETY MATTERS

Psychological safety, put simply, is "the belief that one can speak up without risk of punishment or humiliation."[*] Because reverse mentoring requires vulnerability on the part of both mentees and mentors, it's imperative that each party feels psychologically safe before they enter into the relationship. If not, they may shut down, become defensive, and/or keep quiet if something makes them uncomfortable, which could lead to resentment, fear, anger, and, potentially, a worsening of the problem at hand. Therefore, it's important that HR commit to the following set of parameters before mentors and mentees meet:

- **Conversations are to remain confidential unless explicitly agreed otherwise:** Though you want to encourage mentors and mentees to share as much within their sessions as they feel comfortable, both parties should understand not to share any information outside the relationship without the express permission of the other person. Any party that violates this confidentiality will be held accountable.

- **Either party is free to answer—or not answer—any question asked of them without any repercussion:** Mentees should think critically about what questions

* Amy C. Edmondson and Mark Mortensen, "What Psychological Safety Looks Like in a Hybrid Workplace," *Harvard Business Review*, April 19, 2021, https://hbr.org/2021/04/what-psychological-safety-looks-like-in-a-hybrid-workplace.

they want to ask to get the most out of the relationship and must respect a mentor's declination to answer. Mentors should decide what they are and are
not comfortable sharing and feel empowered to set
boundaries if the mentee asks about an off-limits
subject.

- **HR will provide support throughout the relationship:** With the exception of a pre-scheduled check-in
with all participants, HR should leave participants
alone after they've started meeting. That said, they
should make it clear that they are available if anyone
needs help, has a question, or wants to discuss their
well-being with a neutral third party.

I will share more specifics on how to do each of these
things over the next four chapters, but for now just know
that these are the absolute minimum requirements to ensure psychological safety. If you feel confident that you
can do this and that your employees will trust you to keep
these promises, then you are ready to set up your reverse
mentoring program.

OUTLINE YOUR OBJECTIVES

Because reverse mentoring is just one component of your
larger DEI scheme, it's important to be clear on how it
can help you meet your objectives. Refer back to the goals
you set and gaps you spotted in Chapter 2. In recent years,

the primary focus of many corporate DEI programs has been on increasing gender, LGBTQ+, and racial diversity across the organization and among leadership. But you may have noticed other or more specific trends in your organization as well.

One example of where traditional views of the workforce can be limiting is that of parental leave, which has, up until recently, been exclusively focused on those who give birth. In 2015 the British government passed legislation that required companies operating in the United Kingdom to offer the ability to split parental (formerly maternity) leave between both parents of the child. This was a step in the right direction, acknowledging that non-birth-giving parents still benefit from having time to bond with their newborns, but it still fell short of including all types of families. Several companies, inside and outside the United Kingdom, have taken their policies a step further, broadening parental leave to support adoption, miscarriage, stillbirth, and surrogacy. One of the most progressive family leave policies comes from media conglomerate Publicis Groupe, which announced in 2021 that, effective immediately, adoptive parents and surrogates would receive the same amount (twenty-six weeks) of paid leave as parents who give birth. They also announced paid leave policies for partners and fathers, those dealing with pregnancy loss (both directly and indirectly through a partner or loved one), and those undergoing fertility treatments as well as a second-leave and gradual return-to-work policy to accommodate parents who need more time for care.* This policy acknowledges the vast diversity of experiences new parents may have and thus ensures that no parent is penalized at work for the choices they make for their families.

While the United States lags far behind as the only developed country without federally mandated parental leave, certain states like California, New Jersey, Rhode Island, and New York have adopted more progressive policies to ensure that parents can take the critical time they need to bond with a new child and/or recover from pregnancy and childbirth. In addition, many private companies have realized the need for (and competitive advantage in) offering generous parental leave benefits. For example, Amazon offers twenty weeks of paid maternity leave and six weeks of paid paternity leave. The company also allows new moms to work part-time while they adjust to returning to a full-time schedule. Procter and Gamble offers sixteen weeks of paid maternity leave (for both birth and adoptive mothers) and also allows parents to take up to a year off through a combination of paid and unpaid time off.[†]

Of course, official policy is one thing, but environment and culture is another. Across the globe, research has shown that women who take more time out of the

---

* Zoe Wickens, "Publicis Groupe UK Launches Family Policies," *Employee Benefits*, July 29, 2021, https://employeebenefits.co.uk/publicis-groupe-uk-launches -family-policies/.

† Emily Cavanagh, "10 of the Best Companies for New Parents, Including Amazon, Microsoft, and Freddie Mac," *Insider*, February 19, 2020, https://www.insider .com/the-10-best-companies-for-new-parents-according-glassdoor-reviews-2020-2.

workforce to care for their children often suffer setbacks at work, including slower advancement up the career ladder and less pay over time.* Consider how your formal policies like parental leave affect your employees.

START SMALL

If you have a large organization and/or if you see major gaps in several groups, you may be tempted to involve the entire leadership team in your reverse mentoring program right from the outset or ensure that all underrepresented demographics are represented in the initial cohort of mentors. Ahead of launching a full program, however, it is always best to start with a small pilot so you are able to test and learn quickly. This will make it easier to start and manage a program, allowing you to gather feedback and make any necessary adjustments before rolling the program out to a wider group of participants. When you're dealing with people's identities, emotions, and careers, you want to develop a strategy that seriously considers the potential consequences of getting things wrong. Commit to focusing on the group where you see the biggest gaps and then plan to expand from there. This will help make your selection and matching process more efficient while also making it easier for you to track progress in those areas.

---

* Ivona Hideg, Anja Krstic, Raymond Trau, and Tanya Zarina, "Do Longer Maternity Leaves Hurt Women's Careers?" *Harvard Business Review*, September 14, 2018, https://hbr.org/2018/09/do-longer-maternity-leaves-hurt-womens-careers.

WHAT IF YOUR PILOT IS UNSUCCESSFUL?

You should consider your pilot successful if participants, on the whole, provide positive feedback and feel optimistic about the program's ability to create change. However, if you receive largely negative feedback, several members drop out of the program or fail to show up for meetings, or the program is conducted in a way that creates psychological harm, then you should pause continuing the program until you've had time to reflect on what went wrong and take major steps toward improving things in the future. Once you've established a foundation of trust, you can consider restarting the program based on the parameters set forth in Chapter 2.

⟨⟨ ⟩⟩

The size of your organization will determine the appropriate size of the pilot program, but ideally the pilot should include at least ten and no more than twenty participants (five to ten mentees and an equivalent number of mentors). If your company is small and lacks a sufficient number of potential mentees on its leadership team, select a few from the next level of your hierarchy, too. You can scale up your program later on if you decide to continue it, but this is a good starting place to ensure that you can extract meaningful data and compare different mentor and mentee experiences while simultaneously making it easier to contain and correct any issues that arise.

You'll also want to decide the length and parameters of the program. I recommend that each cohort last no less than six but no more than eight months, with participants meeting once a month for sixty to ninety minutes. In my experience working with and studying reverse mentoring programs across a variety of organizations, I've found that this time commitment allows for a meaningful relationship to develop between participants without asking too much from them in terms of time or energy. It's also short enough to allow you to gather, analyze, and report the data from the program so you can adjust as you go and keep your stakeholders apprised of your progress and insights.

THE SELECTION PROCESS

Mentors and mentees have different roles in a reverse mentoring relationship, so you should handle their selection processes differently.

Mentees

Mentees who are eager to participate in the program will be the most likely to reap the benefits because they will naturally be open to learning, making themselves vulnerable, and listening to their mentor with an open heart and mind—with the intention to take some form of action in response to what they learn. You also want to select people with significant decision-making power within your organization as they are in the best position to exert influence on the rest of the company, either directly through their decisions or indirectly because people tend to mimic the behaviors of those in positions of power. Consider people who have championed DEI in the past and who have expressed curiosity about the subject and/or admitted their own ignorance about people from different backgrounds. If this doesn't describe everyone in leadership, don't worry; the more leaders you can get to participate, the more the resisters will get the message that the program is important and the more receptive they will become. This is yet another reason to start off with a small pilot program—so you can gather data and feedback to make a stronger case later on and so you're not pressuring someone to engage in a relationship for which they are unprepared and that they might not take seriously. In 2019 Cambridge University embarked on a reverse mentoring scheme to help senior academics and managers understand systemic racism from a firsthand perspective. However, the mentors from the pilot reported that the mentees were not taking this work seriously and expressed feeling an undue amount of stress as a result. "It's not been my experience that many heads of departments and colleges really want to hear how bad things are," said Priya Gopal, a senior academic on Cambridge's English faculty. "There is a culture of not taking race seriously."* The university was right to stop the scheme at this point as they realized that they had more work to do

---

* David Batty, "Cambridge May Drop BAME Mentoring of White Academics," *The Guardian*, March 14, 2020, https://www.theguardian.com/education/2020/mar/14/cambridge-may-drop-bame-mentoring-of-white-academics.

in laying a foundation of trust and a commitment to DEI and, most importantly, to ensure psychological safety for those, specifically mentors, taking part.

Mentors

Because mentors will generally not have as much power as their mentees, they might not feel as readily comfortable participating, especially if they come from a demographic group that is underrepresented in your organization. People from marginalized groups are often very sensitive to the way they are perceived. They're acutely aware of discrimination, bias, stereotypes, and microaggressions and may fear being singled out, especially at work. The simple act of asking them to be a mentor forces you to both acknowledge their minority status and highlight a personal characteristic that should, in a perfect world, not matter in their job. Couple this with the fact that you're asking them to have vulnerable—potentially challenging and highly emotional—conversations with someone who holds more authority than them, and there are myriad opportunities to make them feel psychologically unsafe. For this reason, HR should take certain precautions when selecting mentors.

The easiest way is to let would-be mentors self-select by asking people to volunteer to participate. Announce to the company that you're launching a reverse mentoring program and encourage people to apply. Be sure to specify what characteristics you're looking for and why and outline the requirements of the program. Make sure to emphasize that both mentors and mentees will receive training (more on this later) so mentors don't opt out simply because they worry that they'll be unprepared.

Generally, you want to cast as wide a net as possible to ensure the best applicant pool. But if your organization is very large, you might want to limit the scope of recruitment for the sake of simplicity. If you employ 50,000 people around the globe, you'll likely end up with hundreds, if not thousands, of interested mentors. If you can only choose ten, you'll end up wasting a lot of your and those applicants' time as a result. Where one group or department has a leader who is an active advocate of the concept of reverse mentoring, limiting the pilot to that area could be an excellent opportunity to demonstrate reverse mentoring's potential efficacy within the organization. Another suggestion is to put a call out to your high-potential individuals to see whether they would be interested in participating. If or when you decide to expand the program, you can consider opening it up to all levels and locations.

Though, in the past, pairings would have been limited by geographic location, the mass adoption of virtual conferencing software during the COVID-19 pandemic has made it possible to connect with people who work in vastly different locations and departments. If you're casting a wide search, consider matching your mentees with mentors from different countries or cities or in vastly different roles. For example, if the CEO in Europe has lost touch with the experiences and challenges of being on the front line, you may match them with a frontline worker in the United States. As long as the match is based primarily on the core demographic that will help you improve your DEI, the more diversity of background or experience, the better.

Beyond demographics, the ideal mentor is someone who can articulate their lived experience as well as serve as a representative of the group(s) with which they identify. They can share their own stories as well as stories they've heard from others from a personal yet fact-based perspective. Someone who has demonstrated maturity and professionalism in the workplace and can have difficult conversations without letting their emotions take over makes an ideal candidate. They should also be someone who has expressed interest in advancing within the company and whom the company sees value in retaining. Such people are more likely to take the program seriously than someone who will likely be moving on soon.

It's possible that you already have someone or a few people in mind who fit this description. In that case, I recommend reaching out to them directly and encouraging them to apply if they're interested and feel comfortable. Let managers know to do the same thing if they think someone on their team would be a good fit. People love to feel acknowledged and appreciated, so even if someone still declines to participate, the simple act of communicating their importance to the company can, on its own, potentially impact their feelings about the company—and about themselves.

When you do reach out, make it clear that they are by no means *required* to participate and that HR and the company will not question their decision. You should also make it clear that they will receive training prior to the first mentoring session so they understand that they will be prepared. Let them know that they will have guardrails in place to keep them on track and someone in HR to whom they can turn for additional support.

MAKING THE MATCH

Once you've narrowed down your list of mentors, you'll want to consider who will make the best match for your cohort of mentees. The most important thing is to match a mentee with a mentor from outside their department. This not only improves the likelihood that the mentor will feel safe being candid, but it also deepens the level of diversity at play.

You should also take into account the mentee's particular gaps in knowledge. In some cases, the mentee may be self-aware enough to tell you this directly. A white woman may acknowledge that she has limited experience around people of color; a man may realize he's never had a female boss or worked with women in leadership positions. If they aren't willing or able to acknowledge this, then it will be up to you—with the aid of outside help if necessary—to discern the mentee's needs based on their experience at the company. What gaps exist among the mentee's peer group? What is the demographic breakdown of their direct reports and hires? Have they made any comments or received any complaints that suggest bias or ignorance? If necessary, have a conversation with individual mentees during the matching process to ascertain any specific concerns they may have.

Once you've made the matches, I advise asking a trusted colleague to independently review your selections and rationale to ensure that they are valid and you haven't overlooked anything that might impact the mentoring relationship. Once you've done this, you can inform the mentors and mentees of their partner. Start by reaching out to them separately to let them know with whom they've been matched and give them a little background information on the other person. You can then choose to introduce them directly, or you can wait until after you've scheduled their training. You can also choose to facilitate a short face-to-face meeting so the participants don't have to worry about the normal anxiety that comes with meeting someone for the first time at the initial mentoring session.

Regardless of when or how you make the introduction, make it clear that they should not schedule their first meeting until after they've completed their training. Ideally, you should schedule this around the same time as you make the introductions so there isn't a lot of lag time between the introduction and the first session.

TRAINING AND ONBOARDING

Before the first mentoring session, you'll need to train all mentors and mentees on the program. For the most part, the participants should control the process so they can figure out what suits them and their particular relationship, but providing guidelines and structure will give them a foundation on which to build. Training will also help to provide safety because the participants will feel more confident and supported in the process knowing that they're at least somewhat prepared and that there is someone at the company available to assist if necessary. Ask the mentors if there are any subjects or areas about which they feel uncomfortable speaking. You can then relay that information to the mentee and avoid a potentially awkward or very sensitive conversation later on.

Try to train all the mentors together, both because it's more efficient and also because it allows them to share and discuss any concerns they have as a group in advance of the first mentoring meeting. It also allows them to connect with one another so they don't feel isolated, as though they're embarking on this journey alongside peers instead of on their own.

As mentees will likely have more complicated schedules, you'll probably have to set up one-on-one training sessions with each of them. An advantage of this is that it gives mentees a space to be vulnerable, ask questions, and express feelings that they may not be comfortable sharing in front of others, especially other leaders at the company.

Regardless, you'll want to cover certain subjects in each training session:

Both Mentor and Mentee Training

- Expectations (how frequently and how long to meet, etiquette, feedback, etc.)
- Confidentiality (what information can be shared outside of the meeting, what information can be brought into the meeting from outside parties, how to clarify expectations with one another, etc.)
- How to get the most out of a meeting
- Opting out of answering questions

Mentor Training

- Setting and maintaining boundaries (what topics are or are not comfortable being discussed, what to do if your mentee asks about an "off-limits" subject, and when to seek assistance from HR)
- Record-keeping (how to keep a record of topics discussed without spending too much time writing during the meeting)
- What, if any, topics are off-limits

Mentee Training

- How to ask questions while maintaining boundaries
- How to use what you've learned

For more information on each of these subjects, please refer to Chapters 4 and 5, which provide guidelines for mentees and mentors, respectively, and Chapter 6, which covers how to run a mentoring meeting.

OVERSIGHT

After the training is over and you've introduced mentors and mentees to one another, you'll want to step aside and let them manage the rest of the process on their own. The more HR micromanages the relationship, the less authentic it will feel, and the more difficult it will be for mentors and mentees to establish the heartfelt, genuine connections that break down barriers and lead to personal growth and breakthroughs. Still, you'll want to check in at key points along the way to ensure that you can address any issues or concerns before they become more serious. Even if you've matched highly competent and responsible individuals with one another, you're dealing with extremely sensitive topics that, despite participants' best intentions, can potentially lead to discomfort.

I recommend checking in three times during each reverse mentoring cohort:

After the second session, reach out to all participants to see how things are going. Many companies are inclined to check in halfway through a program like this, but in my work with clients, I've found that two sessions in is ideal. By this point, mentors and mentees will have met twice, which means they should have enough information to provide helpful feedback, but you will still have at least four sessions left in the program to course-correct if required. You could arrange another group session for mentors, but for mentees you may need to schedule one-on-one time again. Alternatively, if several of your mentees already meet regularly for other reasons, you could ask them to include you on an existing agenda, for instance as part of a leadership team meeting, so they have the opportunity to share their experiences with one another without having to carve out additional time in their day.

Ask all participants:

- What is working well?
- What could be improved?
- What have you learned?
- What has been rewarding?
- What has been challenging?
- What has been transformative?
- Do you feel safe talking to your mentor or mentee? If not, why not?
- What advice would you give the next cohort of mentors and mentees?

After the fourth session, check in and understand how to focus the final phase of the relationship.

After the final mentoring session, send out a survey to all participants asking for their feedback and observations.

The survey should include the same questions as above, plus additional reflective questions about the process and what could be better so you can continuously improve the program, cohort by cohort. In addition to the survey, schedule two closing sessions, one for all the mentors and the other for all the mentees, to reflect on the process and discuss things learned in a facilitated environment. If the logistics allow, then a joint session with the entire cohort is a nice touch to close the program and an additional opportunity for these groups to learn from one another.

SHARING RESULTS

Once you've collected feedback and insights, you'll want to share the results with the rest of the organization. Regular communication will promote transparency and keep people apprised of progress, which will further signal your overall commitment to DEI. Depending on the results, it should also help spark interest and curiosity in participating in the program, assuming that you choose to continue it. The most important goal of these communications, though, is to take what's been learned within the mentoring relationship and apply it to the organization as a whole by expanding conversations around DEI and how the company can address the needs of marginalized groups.

There are three broad types of regular communication I recommend: company-wide communication,

communication within the leadership team, and communication with employee resource groups (ERGs).

Company-Wide Communication

Include reverse mentoring as part of any regular DEI updates you send to employees, executives, and/or your board
of directors. At the very least, the latest updates and takeaways from the program should appear in quarterly updates
and annual reports, alongside financial, sales, marketing,
business development, or product updates that provide a
snapshot of the health and progress of the company. This
not only allows people to see how the program is faring,
but further signals the organization's commitment to DEI
as a whole.

At the very least, you'll want to include the number
of people who have or are currently participating in the
program, how long the program has been running, and
how many meetings have been had. If possible, break these
numbers out by department, level, and location and announce any current plans to expand the program so people
can see which areas of the company are participating. I also
recommend naming the current mentors and mentees for
increased transparency. Naming the mentees will demonstrate that leadership is taking DEI seriously and is willing
to humble themselves to learn about their marginalized
groups. Naming mentors allows other individuals to seek
them out if they're curious about the program and/or want

to share their own perspectives. When I first participated in a reverse mentoring program with Craig Kreeger, the CEO of my employer, Virgin Atlantic, several people from similar backgrounds to mine shared their experiences with me and expressed their hopes for change in the company. This allowed me to gain an even greater understanding of the issues at work, and I used those to inform the conversations I had with Craig. Based on this experience, I also realized the importance of having a transparent selection process, as people often want to know why certain individuals are selected to participate and not others and may grow resentful if they feel they were passed over.

You should also use these opportunities to share any wins you've had with the program. Did an insight revealed during a mentoring session spark a larger conversation that led to an investigation or policy change? What sorts of positive feedback have you received from mentors or mentees? If they're willing, feel free to quote participants about their experiences as a way to further humanize the program.

Communication with the Leadership Team

Though leaders who participate in reverse mentoring often report being changed by the experience, the real goal of these programs is not to change individuals but to shift the culture of the entire organization to one that embodies inclusivity. Eventually, you'll want all leaders to participate in the program, but leaders can also benefit from hearing about the experiences of others.

The most effective way to encourage this is to schedule—or ask mentees to schedule—time during meetings to share their experiences and the knowledge they've gleaned with other members of the leadership team as well as anyone else with whom they work. They can use this time to share whatever they feel is most relevant or impactful while maintaining the confidentiality of their mentor as outlined in their training. What has their mentor's experience at the company been like? What challenges have they faced? How do the company's policies and procedures affect them differently from others at the organization? Is there a particular program or policy for which this group of people is responsible that has the power to affect a specific group's experience?

For example, a company I consulted with was in the process of launching a Pride campaign when an executive received feedback from their mentor (a member of the LGBTQ+ community) that they and several of their colleagues were uncomfortable with the campaign. They were also upset that the leadership team—comprised entirely of cisgender heterosexuals—had not consulted with anyone from their community before putting it together. The mentee took their mentor's concerns to the rest of the leadership team, who decided to change the campaign with the input of the LGBTQ+ employees. This is exactly the type of change we're looking for: meaningful action as a result of leaning into experience and perspective.

Communication with Employee Resource Groups

Employee resource groups are formal networks of individuals from specific backgrounds within a company that provide advice, mentorship, networking, training, and other resources to help traditionally underrepresented groups advance in their careers. If your organization already has an employee resource program, you can lean on members of those groups as both sources of information for the reverse mentoring program and venues for discussions about key findings from mentoring sessions. If you already have a strong underlying DEI program, you should already have a process for working with ERGs that can be applied to the reverse mentoring program. If not, there are a few best practices to keep in mind.

Given that you want to select mentors who have expressed interest in helping the company improve diversity, there's a high likelihood that at least some of them will already participate in ERGs. If that's the case, encourage them to discuss the program with other members and bring the group's insights and concerns to bear in their conversations. Could the mentee provide feedback or help with an issue the ERG has been working on, or would getting their buy-in improve the odds that the issue gets the attention it needs? Are there particular concerns that the members of the ERG have repeatedly voiced that the mentee may not be aware of but should be?

It's also possible that information shared within a reverse mentoring conversation may bring to light an issue that the ERG could help address. Though many of the experiences shared within these sessions may only reflect the mentor's individual lived experience, there may be issues that come up that potentially affect other employees of the company. For example, a leader at one of my clients was being mentored by an individual with a mobility disability. They revealed some of the challenges that they faced simply navigating around the workplace. Policies and procedures were in place to ensure that required adjustments for individuals could be made, however the actual practicalities of enforcing the policy were very unclear. In fact in this case, when the leader spoke with them, HR themselves struggled to articulate the process. On further investigation it became clear that because requests were few and far between, there wasn't a specific person employed to manage accessibility and therefore it was left to whoever received the request. The leader recognized that they had only understood the lived experience from one individual and needed to understand what else could be hindering individuals with a disability. They discussed these questions with HR and raised a formal request to the network focused on disability to engage them in a review of policies and procedures so the company could provide the right level of support. In addition, after the group's response revealed a multitude of issues that needed to be remedied, they hired one person full-time to work through these issues while also proactively managing the needs of this group going forward.

EMPOWERED ERGs

It is important to honestly assess the power of your ERGs.

- How empowered are they to drive decisions and create policy?
- How supported are they by the leaders within the business to ensure that their views are heard and incorporated?
- How much does the business lean into the lived experiences of these individuals to ensure the best outcome for the business?
- How are ERGs used as a business resource?

If your organization doesn't yet have ERGs that cover the full spectrum of needs in your organization, think carefully about how you can welcome and encourage the views of your underrepresented population in a safe and authentic way.

⟨⟨ ⟩⟩

WHEN TO HIRE A CONSULTANT

If you're new to reverse mentoring, if your DEI program is in its infancy, or if HR lacks the internal capabilities to sufficiently run and manage the program, you may benefit from bringing in an external consultant to help you set up and/or run the scheme. Even if you require outside help, however, HR should never outsource the program entirely. In order to feel safe, employees need to feel that there is someone they can turn to internally if necessary. Besides, the sustainability of the program relies on HR being actively involved.

There are several ways a consultant can help. For starters, they can assist HR in identifying and matching candidates for the program if you'd like an expert's objective opinion on who would be most successful. A consultant can also assist with the pre-program training, either by running the training themselves or by training HR to conduct it. If the former, the person overseeing the program internally should be present to address any employee concerns outside the consultant's purview and to learn what is expected of participants and what potential points of discomfort may exist. Consultants can also help you analyze your overall DEI strategy to see how a reverse mentoring program can best fit within it and review any communications before you send them out. If you choose to work with a consultant, it's important to use them as an educator, not a contractor. You are hiring them to teach you what you need to know to eventually take over the program yourself, not to do the job for you.

In my work as a consultant, clients have sometimes asked me to sit in on mentoring sessions. Though I can understand why HR might want a neutral third-party present to mediate any conflicts, this will actually undermine psychological safety. Mentors and mentees will likely feel uncomfortable sharing their vulnerabilities with one stranger, let alone two, and requiring a third party may suggest to the participants that the company doesn't trust them to behave like adults. Trust your people, trust the process, and trust yourself to handle any challenges that arise.

WHEN TO SCALE

Given the amount of diversity that exists in the world and the fact that leadership will continue to turn over, the best reverse mentoring programs are ongoing, consistent, and woven into the fabric of the organization, just like a regular mentoring program. If you deem the pilot program a success, you'll no doubt want to continue and expand beyond it. Don't be discouraged if your first attempt was imperfect, or even if some participants had a negative experience. As long as you have committed to doing better and, overall, people feel safe participating, you'll likely benefit from continuing the program beyond the pilot. If, however, the results of the pilot reveal that the organization is not able and/or willing to act on what they have learned, I recommend pausing the full rollout until more work has been done to increase the level of trust and build momentum to move forward in an effective manner.

Though you'll likely want to wait until the pilot is completed so you can collect and analyze the data from it, if the first few sessions are successful and there is a lot of interest in the program among potential mentors and mentees (and you have the resources to properly manage a bigger cohort), consider expanding the program sooner rather than later.

As with any initiative, you'll want to consistently measure its impact and track your progress toward your DEI goals with the results of the program. As time goes on and you feel more comfortable running the program, you can expand it to be more sophisticated, potentially addressing the needs of many different groups at once instead of focusing on just one or two aspects of diversity. Continue the program at least until all leaders within the organization have had an opportunity to participate as mentees, though if you reach this milestone and still see areas in need of improvement, you could consider cycling through the leadership team again, matching them with mentors from different backgrounds from their last one to further broaden their perspectives and expand the conversations around diversity at the company. For example, while most companies are still focused on improving gender and racial representation, more sophisticated companies have moved beyond these areas to recognize that diversity comes in many forms, far beyond what we can readily perceive. Here are just a few areas beyond race and gender that affect a person's experience, particularly in the workplace:

- Sexual orientation
- Marital status
- Parental status
- Neurodiversity
- Non-childcare caregiving responsibilities (aging parents, sick family members, etc.)
- Hormones (menopause, hormone therapies for gender transition, etc.)
- Pregnancy
- Disability, disfigurement, or chronic illness
- Mental health
- Immigration status
- Extroversion versus introversion
- Veteran status
- Socioeconomic or financial status (working multiple jobs, paying off debt, etc.)

Choosing to embark on a reverse mentoring journey can be scary as an HR representative. For generations, HR departments have discouraged "unnecessary" conversations about personal experiences at work, but now we're seeing how that attitude has limited our ability to grow as individuals and organizations. It silences the importance of identity, it shames difference, and it minimizes creativity. We are who we are, and we cannot—nor should we—ask people to ignore that. Vulnerability, showing up as our whole selves without fear or judgment, is a powerful tool for growth. As long as you put the proper guardrails in place and approach the program with humility, compassion, and a commitment to change, your chances of success—and that your employees and leaders will benefit—are high.

CHAPTER FOUR

MENTEE RESPONSIBILITIES

Congratulations! You've been selected to participate as a mentee in a reverse mentoring program. You're about to embark on a journey that, if successful, will help you grow as a leader by giving you the tools to effectively lead diverse teams and build inclusive relationships. The insights you gain have tremendous potential to help you shape the way your organization delivers on diversity, equity, and inclusion and will also influence the way you interact with those around you, both personally and professionally. Reverse mentoring offers a unique opportunity for you to learn while simultaneously connecting with others and helping them reach their goals. This is an exciting moment.

In order to get the most out of this experience, there are several things you should do to prepare, as well as guidelines and best practices to keep in mind as you move forward in your mentoring relationship.

YOUR ROLE AS A MENTEE

If you're in a leadership position at your organization, you are likely used to assuming authority and having people listen to and learn from you. You may even have served as a mentor at some point in your professional journey, offering advice and insights to help a younger, less experienced person further their career or develop their leadership skills.

Now, prepare for the difficult part. In a reverse mentoring relationship, you are being asked to assume the role of mentee, the student who has shown up to learn. In this instance, you may currently have very little experience or knowledge of the topic at hand. By agreeing to participate, you are acknowledging your lack of knowledge—ignorance even—on certain topics, specifically the issues regarding diversity, equity, and inclusion at your organization. You are most comfortable being in charge and having people defer to your expertise and opinions, but you are now humbling yourself, most likely to a mentor who, under the traditional hierarchy of an organization, holds less power than you. In addition, you and your mentor will be discussing topics that you may have never discussed with anyone, let alone a colleague you barely know. Your mentor will share some of the most personal aspects of their life and lived experiences with you while inviting you to share details about your own life you may not be used to disclosing in a professional setting.

At times, this may feel uncomfortable, but that is exactly the point. Reverse mentoring is designed to foster empathy and understanding between individuals with different identities, backgrounds, and experiences in an effort to create awareness and inspire change around issues that affect members of marginalized groups in our society. This requires being honest about our biases, confronting our assumptions and privileges, and admitting when we've made mistakes or harmed other people in the past (intentionally or not). Without this vulnerability, you will never be able to accept reality and do better. Empathy is a muscle: the more you exert it and push it past its limits, the stronger it gets.

To do this, you must begin by embracing your full responsibilities as a mentee. Over the next several months, keep this list in mind as you move through the mentoring relationship:

- Prepare yourself before each session by thinking of topics you want to discuss and/or questions you want to ask.
- Listen actively to what your mentor has to say and express curiosity about their life.

- Share insights with your mentor about your current position, duties, and challenges.
- Admit when you don't know or understand something, and ask questions that help deepen your knowledge.
- Encourage vulnerability by sharing relevant details of your life with your mentor (vulnerability is a two-way street).
- Respect and acknowledge your mentor's experiences, boundaries, and viewpoints.
- Consider how your actions (current and past) and role within the organization impact your mentor's (and others') experience and what you could change to improve that experience.
- Amplify the voice of your mentor by sharing what you've learned about yourself and the organization with other leaders and stakeholders.

BEFORE YOUR FIRST MEETING

Though you want your mentoring sessions to feel as informal as possible, it's important to prepare in advance to ensure that you're entering into the program with the right mindset, attitude, and foundational knowledge. Remember, your mentor is embarking on an incredibly vulnerable and personal journey with you; taking the time to do the following things before your first mentoring session will demonstrate your commitment to them and the process.

Clarify Your Goals

Before your first meeting, it's important to clarify why you're participating and what you hope to achieve from the mentoring relationship. If you've volunteered to be a mentee, you may already have some idea, but it's worth taking the time to check in with yourself to be sure. The more specific you can be with your goals and personal commitment, the more strategic and effective you can be when talking with your mentor.

Think about what you are excited to learn or what you could potentially gain from the process. If you walk in feeling like this is something you're doing to satisfy your boss, to "tick a box" on a training program, or because you think it makes you look like a team player, you will not have a successful partnership and may do more harm than good. Reverse mentoring requires an open mind, open heart, and genuine curiosity about the other person and their lived experiences. Your mentor will sense if you're distracted, bored, disinterested, or disingenuous, which will create tension and a lack of safety. Show your mentor respect by opening yourself up to receive what they have to teach you.

As an exercise to help you do this, ask yourself these questions:

- What do you want to get out of this relationship?
- What are your prior experiences or relationships with people from the same or similar background

as your mentor? Have you ever had a close personal or professional relationship with someone from this background?

- What are the largest gaps in your knowledge and understanding regarding underrepresented groups?
- What assumptions do you have about this underrepresented group? What has influenced your beliefs or assumptions around this group?
- What are some issues at play or feedback you've received from colleagues about how you and/or others in the organization treat people from diverse backgrounds? What might you be able to glean from your mentor to help you address those issues?
- Why is inclusivity important to you? How much change are you willing to make (personally and as a leader in the organization)?
- What role can you play in encouraging diversity, inclusion, and equity at your organization? How much authority do you have and what policies could you influence?
- How prepared are you to listen to and then champion on behalf of your mentor's group(s), even if they're not seated at the decision-making table?
- Who are the change agents on your leadership team, and who are the ones happy with the status quo? Where do you feel you belong on this continuum?
- What do you commit to doing after the program? What does success look like for you?

Do Your Homework

In a traditional mentoring relationship, a mentee wouldn't show up to the meeting without knowing some basic facts about their mentor and the organization. That's because it is not the mentor's job to tell them what they need to know. Rather, it falls to the mentee to figure out what they want to get out of the relationship and use that goal to steer the conversation.

The same goes for reverse mentoring relationships. Before you sit down with your mentor for the first time, get to know their journey at your company. What department are they in? What are their responsibilities? How long have they been there? How many promotions have they received? How has their trajectory mirrored or differed from others at the company? HR should be able to provide you with this information. If available, try to learn some more personal facts about them: whether they are married, have children, etc. However, try not to worry if you do not have a full picture of your mentor before meeting them. This information will come to light during your meetings; in fact, that is the whole point of this relationship.

You should also find out how your mentor prefers to be identified, both as an individual and as a representative of a particular group or groups. Do not assume that you know how someone identifies based on how they appear or present themselves. What are their preferred pronouns? How do they classify their ethnicity and what term(s) do they prefer to use? For example, a person from Puerto Rico may identify as Puerto Rican, Boricua, Taíno, Hispanic, Latinx, American, or some combination thereof. How do they prefer to be referred to in the third person? For example, some people with disabilities reject the phrase "disabled person" in favor of a "person-first" approach, such as "a person with a disability." They might also not consider their condition to be a disability, even though it falls under the legal definition of one. For example, many members of the deaf community consider their inability to hear to be a feature, not a bug—something that forces them to communicate differently but not any less well than those with hearing.

Beyond your mentor's individual experience, take the time to educate yourself about how the groups with which they identify are represented in your organization and society as a whole. If your mentor is a gay Black man, find out how many queer and Black people are currently employed at your organization. How many of them are in leadership positions? How does their tenure at the company compare to people from other groups? How does their representation reflect these groups' representations in your community as a whole? Again, HR should be able to provide you with this information based on previous diversity surveys. Informing yourself on these points in advance, if you haven't already, shows that you are committed to learning and also relieves the burden of educating you on these basic points from your mentor's lap so you can spend more time learning about their personal experiences instead of things you can research on your own.

Best Practices

At your first meeting, you and your mentor will discuss your preferences for scheduling meetings, communication, and confidentiality (see Chapter 6 for more on this). But there are a few guidelines all mentees should keep in mind to ensure a productive relationship.

- **Be punctual:** This should go without saying, but as someone with a lot of responsibilities and demands on your time, you will most certainly be faced with scheduling challenges during the course of your mentoring relationship. But if you continuously show up late, leave early, or cancel meetings at the last minute, not only will you lose the opportunity to benefit from what your mentor has to teach you, but you also signal to them that you don't prioritize this relationship or respect their time. By extension, you communicate to the rest of the organization that you don't consider diversity, equity, and inclusion to be priorities, thus limiting your ability to be an agent of change and potentially sabotaging the larger DEI initiatives at the company. If you absolutely need to cancel, strive to give your mentor plenty of advance notice, and be sure to reschedule immediately. If you're going to be late, make sure to let them know so they're not waiting around idly. The same goes for any follow-up you're expected to do between sessions; deliver on your agreed commitments on time. Common courtesy can go a long way as long as you don't make discourtesy a habit.

- **Inform your assistant:** Because your assistant is likely the person responsible for managing your calendar, let them know that all reverse mentoring meetings should be prioritized and that the time should not be interfered with unless absolutely necessary. Make sure that they prioritize any messages from your mentor while respecting the boundaries of privacy and confidentiality you and your mentor set up in your first meeting (see Chapter 6).

- **Reduce distractions during meetings:** Turn your phone off and put it away while you are meeting with your mentor. If necessary, talk to your assistant about a way to get in touch with you in case of emergencies only, and determine in advance what constitutes an emergency. If you are meeting in the office, use a room that is discreet or, if that's not possible, turn your back to the window or door so you're not distracted by people walking by.

- **Schedule meetings mindfully:** You know when you are most productive and when your energy levels are at their highest. You also know when you are less likely to have your day derailed by an emergency, a delay, or some other stressor. Schedule mentoring meetings with this in mind. Also consider your mentor's schedule, time preferences, and personal commitments. High energy and few interruptions will create the space for a strong relationship to be formed with fruitful discussion, which will benefit both of you.

- **Take notes judiciously:** Mentoring sessions should feel as natural and informal as possible. You want to let conversation flow freely, as if you were having a chat with a friend. Though it's good, even necessary, to record your observations and discoveries from each session, set aside time to do so *after* the meeting so you don't distract from the discussion at hand. An exception would be if you want to take note of key takeaway actions. For instance, if your mentor mentions a program or policy they'd like to change, write it down so you can follow up on it and demonstrate that you are taking it seriously.

 THE FAR-REACHING CONSEQUENCES
OF A DISENGAGED MENTEE

The following individual was part of a pilot reverse mentoring scheme, with an employer of 10,000 individuals. He was an active spokesperson within his immediate team, and he was excited to elevate the conversations and share his views with senior leaders. He was ambitious, keen to make a difference and progress, however he felt he wasn't listened to. This was a great opportunity for him.

> Sadly, the mentee never made themselves available for the process. They constantly had their personal assistant contact me instead of speaking with me. The biggest aha moment was the lack of respect this specific leader had toward their junior colleagues, a complete lack of awareness of how that almost dismissive attitude can impact individuals. This disconnect in behavior, between purporting to support change but then behaving in a contradictory way, causes disappointment and increases the lack of trust which already exists. You begin to wonder: if they are unable to see themselves in you, to relate to you, would one ever be able to flourish within the business?

The mentee's disregard didn't only impact the proposed mentor but other employees as well. When the mentor shared their experience with their colleagues who had been very excited and proud that this individual had been chosen, it further perpetuated the assumptions that the team had about the leadership. For them it reinforced the idea that upper management didn't really care for engagement and that their messages of solidarity and support were all talk and little action. The proposed mentor refrained from volunteering again. The leader, though spoken to, did not reach out to the mentor after receiving this feedback.

Get to Know One Another

Prior to the first official meeting, HR should reach out to both you and your mentor to schedule a short introductory session. This need not be longer than fifteen or twenty minutes and is basically designed to review the scope of the relationship so everyone is on the same page about what is expected.

After this initial introduction but before your first mentoring session, ensure that you schedule some one-on-one time with your mentor directly so you can get acquainted with one another before you begin the hard-hitting work of mentorship. Invite them to lunch or coffee—somewhere informal where you can both feel at ease and focus on each other. There should be no agenda for this meeting other than learning more about one another's lives and pivotal experiences. Stay flexible and informal, but if you sense your mentor is a little shy or uncomfortable opening up—which is possible given your relative positions within the organization—encourage them to share by divulging details about yourself. Go beyond the basic résumé highlights or job-interview questions to share the formative experiences that made you who you are today. How did you end up in this career? What experiences helped shape your perspective on the world? Use these stories as an invitation to your mentor to share their own experiences. Stay curious and focus on building a relationship. When the meeting is over, take note of anything your mentor mentioned that you'd like to follow up on or are curious about. This can be used as the basis for questions during your reverse mentoring sessions.

CONDUCTING A MEETING

Before you delve into these intimate learning sessions, you'll want to set some ground rules for confidentiality, privacy, protocol, and communication. Be sure not to skip this step, as it will provide the foundation for a safe, productive relationship and ensure that there is no ambiguity surrounding your expectations of one another.

Once you've laid this foundation, you should be ready to start asking the questions that will help you grow and change as a leader. Ideally, these conversations will flow naturally, and you and your mentor will develop a rapport that allows each of you to share personal stories, perspectives, and experiences in a way that helps build empathy and understanding while keeping the primary goal of these sessions top of mind—to deepen your views on diversity, equity, and inclusion with an eye toward improving your organization.

There are a few things you as a mentee can do to facilitate these conversations, techniques that allow for vulnerability without letting emotions become overwhelming.

Ask Open-Ended Questions

Leaders often ask questions knowing what answers they want, but in a reverse mentoring relationship, you need to leave yourself open to hearing the unexpected—perhaps uncomfortable—truth about your mentor's lived experiences. To do this, stay away from closed or leading questions, which often prompt people to give a specific type of response. Instead, ask open-ended questions that allow your mentor the space to really consider the answer that is most accurate.

For example, instead of:

Did that experience make you feel angry?

Try:

How did that experience make you feel?

Or, instead of:

Do you feel our organization's policies are discriminatory?

Try:

How do you experience this organization as a place to work?

Practice Active Listening

One of the biggest hurdles to building empathy between individuals is when people talk without actually listening. How many times have you been conversing with someone, and the entire time they're telling a story or sharing an opinion, you're waiting impatiently for them to finish while formulating what you're going to say in response? When we do this, we're so focused on ourselves and what we want to say that we end up missing—or misunderstanding—most of the information being communicated to us. We don't absorb or consider what we're being told and default to what we already know—or think we know—instead of taking the time to understand and reckon with a new perspective. In this instance, we are listening to respond rather than listening to understand. This is why so many debates end with people arguing and being even more entrenched in their own opinions rather than coming to a compromise or mutual understanding.

In order to get the most out of your mentoring sessions, you need to truly *hear* what your mentor is telling you. You can do this through a process known as active listening. Active listening requires you to engage in several key listening skills that allow you to better process information while demonstrating that you are paying attention and showing respect:

- **Pay attention:** Make eye contact with your mentor, focus on what they're actually saying in the moment, and don't worry about feeling the need to respond. Wait for them to finish their thought. Don't interrupt.
- **Withhold judgment:** If your mentor shares an idea or opinion with which you disagree, notice your reaction but wait until they have finished speaking to formulate a response. You may find that the more you listen, the more you naturally come to understand their perspective, even if it challenges a preconceived notion of yours.
- **Clarify:** Don't be afraid to ask your mentor to clarify something if you don't understand or if you missed

some key information. Good listeners gather as much accurate information as possible before responding or making a decision.

- **Validate their feelings:** When people share uncomfortable information with us, our natural response is often to skirt around the discomfort by minimizing the gravity of the situation. As a leader, you may be used to trying to build consensus or defuse conflict, but your role here is not to be a peacemaker; it's to try to appreciate your mentor's lived experiences and how those experiences affect their day-to-day life. You may not have all the facts about an absent party's role, actions, or motivations in a situation, but that doesn't matter; what matters is how your mentor felt after interacting with that person. Avoid phrases like "maybe they didn't mean it that way," "maybe you misunderstood," and "perhaps you are being too sensitive" that dismiss or minimize your mentor's feelings. Instead, opt for validating language or questions such as "How did that make you feel?" or "That must have been very difficult to experience."
- **Summarize:** A great way to show someone that you're listening to them—and to ensure that you are understanding them correctly—is to summarize or repeat back what they tell you. If your mentor tells you a story about being passed over for a promotion in favor of someone less experienced, you might summarize by saying, "Let me make sure I understand.

You had spoken with your manager at last year's review about what you needed to do to qualify for this new position. You did what was asked, but the position was given to someone else at the company with five years less experience and with whom you, personally, have had performance issues in the past. Is that accurate?"*

Encourage Vulnerability by Being Vulnerable

As part of the reverse mentoring arrangement, your mentor is agreeing to share some of their deepest, most personal stories and experiences with you in an effort to help you improve as a leader. This is an incredible commitment, one that proves their willingness to make themselves vulnerable in order to help you (someone they likely barely know), the organization, and other members of the groups with which they identify. When someone opens themselves up to you in this way, you are forced to see them not simply as a colleague or member of a specific race, gender identity, or other demographic group, but as a human being with challenges, hopes, talents, and connections similar to your own. When we learn to see others as we see ourselves, we build tacit empathy: we begin to see *their* struggles as *our* struggles. The issues are no longer theirs and become ours;

---

* Leading Effectively Staff, "Use Active Listening Skills to Coach Others," Center for Creative Leadership, December 2, 2021, https://www.ccl.org/articles/leading -effectively-articles/coaching-others-use-active-listening-skills/.

we become more committed to making changes that improve lives and society as a whole.

But even the most eager and willing mentor may, at least at first, feel awkward sharing these aspects of themselves with you. This may not have anything to do with you as a person but could reflect previous experiences they've had with people who made them feel as though they had to hide certain things in order to be safe. This may include years of changing their identity to feel accepted and minimizing their personal experiences to feel understood. Still, it is now your responsibility to encourage them to be vulnerable with you and to be their authentic self. Otherwise, the relationship will not be effective.

The easiest way to encourage vulnerability is to practice vulnerability. Though you don't want to take the focus away from your mentor by making the conversation about *you*, it can be worthwhile to share some details about your own life as a way to offer them permission to do the same. Although you may have a very different background from your mentor, what are some challenges you've faced in your life? You can also be vulnerable by admitting your ignorance on certain issues, acknowledging previous mistakes that you made, or confessing beliefs that you are actively trying to change. For example, one of my interviewees, whom we'll call Drew, was a mentee in a reverse mentoring program within a global telecoms organization and was being mentored by Michael, a gay white male who had come out to his family only a few months prior. Drew had grown up in a conservative community that believed that homosexuality was aberrant, and even though Drew was only moderately religious, he still didn't understand or support same-sex marriage. When his older brother came out as gay later in life, it caused a huge family divide, and Drew felt that the person he had looked up to had been lying to him his whole life. Listening to Michael share his journey of coming out, Drew finally understood that his brother had been denying a critical part of his identity for a long time and had felt villainized by his church, family, and surrounding society. While many of their family members chose to ostracize his brother, Drew realized that his brother was no less worthy of love from family and friends than he had been before and sought to really understand some of the challenges that he had faced throughout his life. His reverse mentoring relationship was instrumental in building a bridge toward understanding and supporting his brother.

Respect Boundaries

Although your mentor has agreed to be vulnerable with you, there may be certain topics that they simply do not feel comfortable discussing or that trigger emotions that compromise their psychological safety. Your mentor should have communicated this to HR during the matching process, in which case HR should have communicated it to you well in advance of your first mentoring meeting.

No matter how curious you are about these subjects, and no matter how strong your relationship with your mentor becomes, do not under any circumstances violate their trust by bringing up subjects with which they are not comfortable. If, at any point, they become willing to share, they will let you know.

Avoiding off-limits topics may seem obvious, but you may also find that a subject not previously flagged as taboo may set off a negative reaction in your mentor that changes the tone of your conversation. This may happen, for example, if they hadn't previously identified a particular topic as a trigger and therefore didn't think to flag it for HR. If you notice your mentor becoming emotional, ask them if they want to stop the conversation, take a break, or change the subject, and give them as much time as they need to compose themselves before they continue. Given the nature of your conversations, a certain amount of emotion is natural, even expected, but make it clear that your mentor has the power to stop the conversation at any time if it becomes overwhelming.

That said, never stop a conversation if your mentor wants to keep going. A lot of people become uncomfortable watching someone, especially someone they know professionally, cry or get angry, but this discomfort is essential to your learning process. If you feel uncomfortable hearing your mentor talk about or react to something, force yourself to sit with that discomfort and consider why that may be the case. Remember, your level of discomfort in this session is incomparable to the discomfort that they feel living these experiences. If they are okay continuing to talk, you will be okay continuing to listen. Cutting them off or changing the subject in this scenario is a sign of disrespect and closed-mindedness.

Similarly, train yourself to be comfortable with silence. At certain points, your mentor may want to take some time to consider your question before answering, or they may want to compose themselves before continuing to share a difficult story. There is no need to rush, and giving them the space they need to share in the manner that makes them most comfortable will lead to a healthier, more productive, and more mutually beneficial relationship in the long run.

HOW AND WHEN TO COURSE-CORRECT

If you, your mentor, and your organization have set up strong parameters for a safe, inclusive reverse mentoring program, your mentor will hopefully feel comfortable correcting or pointing out any problematic language or behavior that occurs during a meeting. Like you, your mentor understands that you are there to learn, which means that you might make mistakes or need to be educated on proper terminology and conduct. With this in mind, your mentor is empowered to correct you if you make a mistake, and you should be open to receiving such feedback in real time and reflecting on how you can make a personal change after you leave the session.

If your mentor corrects you, thank them for pointing out your mistake and make it clear that you will take that information to heart so you can do better moving forward. If you are confused as to why they corrected you, ask questions to deepen your understanding. Do so respectfully and from a place of curiosity, not from a place of defensiveness. One former mentee described to me how they course-corrected after making a mistake:

I had assumed Gabrielle's heritage was Jamaican. I had made this assumption because in the area surrounding our office, there was a large Jamaican population. I started our conversation describing how I loved Jamaica, Bob Marley, and curried goat. She looked really uncomfortable, and I couldn't figure out why. About ten minutes into the conversation, she asked to pause and said "Amy, I think we need to track back to the start of our conversation. I appreciate that you were trying to build a rapport, however just because I am Black and the community that surrounds us is Jamaican, it really offended me that you assumed that I was, too. You didn't even ask me the question or let me speak first. You just made an assumption." Whelp. I could feel the color creeping up my neck and cheeks as the embarrassment of what I had just said sunk in. I had prepped for this session. The first thing I had written down in my notes is not to make assumptions. So how did I forget my prep so quickly to start with such a massive one?! Around twenty-four hours after the

session, I reached out to Gabrielle to thank her for being comfortable in challenging me and giving me a real,
live teachable moment. I apologized, acknowledged the
offense that I had caused her, and vowed that I would do
better going forward, committing to be more conscious
with my biases and words.

It is important to start your sessions with the right intention, but it is also important to remember that intentions are useless unless backed up with action. In Amy's case
it was clear that she did some preparation on the surface but
had not fully internalized the lesson.

Of course, there may come a time when you say something problematic or offensive but your mentor doesn't
immediately speak up. They may hesitate because they are
nervous, are triggered, or need some time to formulate a
response. If you notice their body language, facial expres-
sion, or tone of voice change and sense that something is
amiss, ask them about it. You may say something like "Was
something I said offensive?" "Would you like to discuss
what's wrong?" "I'd like to pause this conversation so you
can share what's on your mind," or anything else that invites them to offer feedback without being confrontational
or assuming that you know what's going on.

Keep in mind that you are the student, and your mentor
is the teacher. Good teachers use their students' mistakes
as opportunities to teach, not to shame or ridicule. Your
mentor has volunteered their time to instruct you because

they want you to learn, grow, and develop as a leader. Open yourself up to this process, and thank them for their time, consideration, and insight when they correct you.

USING WHAT YOU LEARN

If your reverse mentoring relationship is successful, you will gain an amazing amount of insight and information, but that knowledge is useless if you don't apply it beyond the scope of your sessions. In order to utilize this information most effectively, make a habit of certain practices.

Reflect and Record

Following each session, set aside some time to reflect on your conversation and what you learned. Keep a journal where you write down what you learned and the insights you found most valuable.

- What surprised you?
- How have your perspectives changed?
- What did you learn that you hadn't fully understood before?
- How can these new insights affect how you behave and interact with others from certain groups?
- How does it change your outlook as a leader?
- Being mindful of confidentiality, what are you able to share with your peers?

- How will this inform your business strategy?
- What changes should you propose?

Writing things down will help you keep track of your progress and give you a document to refer to when it comes time to share the results of your meetings with others. That leads us to the second step . . .

Share

As a leader, it is your responsibility to share what you've learned from your mentor with other members of the leadership team and key players in your organization. Hopefully, every manager and executive at your company will participate in their own reverse mentoring program, but every individual will walk away with different insights that, when shared, can lead to powerful breakthroughs. At least once a month (or however frequently you and your mentor meet), add a discussion of your DEI insights to any relevant meeting agendas. Use these times as an opportunity to share what you've learned and discuss any policies, procedures, or initiatives that the group in question could address. One of my interviewees, Amir, a business director from a multinational bank, shared that when he relocated to the United States from the Middle East, he really struggled to understand the dynamics of the different cultures. There was a course on cultural acclimatization, however it didn't cover all the dynamics at play among the various demographic groups, so HR suggested pairing Amir up with two individuals with different characteristics to help him to gain a deeper insight into these groups. He discovered that the cultural dynamics in the Middle East were very different to those in the United States and that there was even a distinction between northern and southern states. From this new vantage point, he was able to lead from a place of greater understanding and sensitivity. He was able to share insights with the leadership team on what he had learned, which ended up being helpful for them, too. Even though many of them had grown up in the United States, some of them had not fully appreciated the differences that existed until they were pointed out.

In addition, include key insights with any regular company or department updates you share with the organization, such as quarterly or annual reports. Depending on the nature of the communication, you might work with other members of the leadership team, other mentees, and/or HR to figure out what to include.

Implement

At some point in your relationship, you and your mentor should discuss any policies or procedures at your organization that present challenges for certain groups. If this does not come up naturally, be sure to ask your mentor about it before your final meeting. Though it takes time to build a fully inclusive culture, you might be able to change some current policies or programs to be less discriminatory right away. For example, your mentor could point out that the company dress code for frontline employees discriminates against certain minority groups by forbidding certain hairstyles, hair coverings, or other adornments. Or you may lack all-gender restrooms. Sharing insights like these with HR so they can work with the appropriate employee resource group (if one is in place) to conduct an audit and brainstorm appropriate solutions is crucial, as is your involvement to ensure that change happens. Your sponsorship and continued commitment are vital here.

Respect Your Mentor's Privacy

You and your mentor can ensure one another's privacy by deciding what is and what is not okay to share outside of your conversations. Though your insights and experiences are yours to share, consider how doing so might impact your mentor's privacy when deciding how and with whom to share. For example, if your mentor tells you why they think they were discriminated against in being overlooked for a promotion, you don't want that information getting back to the decision-maker involved because it could lead to issues for them and your mentor. If your mentor discloses something you feel that HR should know about, discuss with your mentor the best way to handle that information. In many cases, people from underrepresented groups are often skeptical of the procedures and policies in place to protect employees from discriminatory behavior, often because they lack faith that any meaningful change or consequence will happen. However, as a leader, it is your responsibility to ensure that all individuals are protected and feel safe and respected coming to work, so you may not be able to turn a blind eye to information that comes to light in these sessions.

Most importantly, let the experience of learning about your mentor's lived experiences change you. As you move through the world—both personally and professionally—consider how identity has affected their lived experiences, including their ability to work, advance in their careers, and feel included. What systems exist that make it more difficult for some people to live safe and prosperous lives than others? How do these systems influence your organization? What changes will you make to create an equitable, inclusive environment?

"I came to the table with a curiosity to learn more and knowing that, to truly manage people, you need to understand the barriers and challenges that they may face," said Mark, a senior leader within UK government. "I have left this experience with a deeper level of empathy for others. We live in a society and particular ecosystems that 'do not have the time' to look for different views. Reverse mentoring is a great way to formalize bringing different seniorities, backgrounds, and demographics together and learn about different perspectives."

CHAPTER FIVE

MENTOR RESPONSIBILITIES

Congratulations! You have been selected to be a mentor as part of your organization's effort to promote more inclusion, better representation, and a stronger sense of belonging among underrepresented, misunderstood, or marginalized groups. Your selection demonstrates that your company believes that you have specific skills and insights that can help a key decision-maker grow into a more effective and empathetic leader. It also shows that they trust you to work and interact with your mentee professionally and positively even though you may hold a very different position from them within the company. Your organization believes that you have what it takes to make this relationship successful and fruitful, but if you've never participated in a reverse mentoring program before, you might feel unprepared, perhaps even apprehensive, about what's to come. That's understandable, which is why this chapter will walk you through your roles and responsibilities as a mentor while outlining best practices to ensure a good outcome for all.

YOUR ROLE AS A MENTOR

Just as in a traditional mentoring relationship, your job as a mentor is to use your wisdom, skills, and experience to enhance the understanding of your mentee. The difference, of course, is that while you hold the position of authority within the reverse mentoring relationship, your mentee is likely more senior, perhaps significantly so, to you within the organization as a whole. At first, you might feel nervous or intimidated by this dynamic, but remember that your mentee has entered into the same contract as you: you are there to teach, and they are there to learn. Your job description, résumé, tenure, and experience level are generally irrelevant within the context of these conversations. What matters is your lived experience as a member of a traditionally marginalized group (or groups) and what insights you may pass on to your mentee by sharing and discussing these experiences.

As a mentor, your roles include the following:

- Be patient and withhold judgment in order to create a safe, constructive environment for your mentee to build empathy and learn.

- Share significant moments, stories, and challenges as a member of the group(s) with which you identify and explain how they have shaped your perspectives and experiences in your life and career.

- Develop your mentee's understanding of inclusion and how the lack of it affects your experience as an individual and as an employee of your organization.

- Help your mentee reframe their perspective with an eye toward prioritizing diversity, equity, and inclusion in both their personal and professional lives.

- Correct and/or challenge your mentee when necessary in order to educate them and help them grow as a leader and an ally.

WHAT KIND OF MENTOR DO YOU WANT TO BE?

Though the prospect of sharing your most personal stories and discussing your lived experiences with someone you barely know may feel uncomfortable, this process is integral to the reverse mentoring program because it's how your mentee will learn. Reverse mentoring works because it uses intimate, first-person stories to build empathy between two people who often come from very different backgrounds. When leaders have empathy for all the people they serve, not just those who look like them or come from similar backgrounds, they make decisions that are more likely to benefit everyone instead of just a select few. When they understand how their choices impact others, they are better able to evaluate those choices and, if necessary, correct past mistakes. Your stories, therefore, have the power to literally change lives for the better.

To overcome any initial discomfort you may have in making yourself vulnerable, it can be useful to consider what legacy you want to leave behind—as an individual, as a representative of a particular group or groups, and as an employee of your organization. If you're not sure, try asking yourself these questions:

- What have my lived experiences taught me that I'd like others to understand?
- What would I like to see change to make things easier or more equitable for those who share my identity or background?
- What would have made my career journey easier?
- What additional support do the groups with which I identify need in order to level the playing field within our organization?
- What do these groups need from an ally within leadership? How are we represented at leadership level?

When considering these questions, you should also ask yourself whether you feel comfortable speaking up on behalf of other people who share your identity(ies) or if you want to limit what you share to your own firsthand observations and experiences. If you have spent time studying or advocating for certain issues, causes, or groups, you may be equipped to offer a perspective that blends your own experiences with those of other people. You may even feel comfortable speaking up on behalf of groups with whom you don't directly identify if you have close personal experience with members of these groups and a solid understanding of the challenges they face. For example, you may identify as heterosexual but have a sibling who identifies as LGBTQ+, or you may have a close friend who has a disability. If you've spoken to them about their lived experiences and/or observed their struggles firsthand, you might be able to use the empathy you have for them to inform conversations with your mentee.

BEST PRACTICES

At your first meeting, you and your mentee will discuss your preferences for scheduling meetings, communication, and confidentiality (see Chapter 6 for more on this). But there are a few guidelines all mentors should keep in mind to ensure a productive relationship:

- **Scheduling:** This should go without saying, but be sure to show up on time to all meetings. Depending on your mentee's position within the company, they likely have a packed schedule but have been asked to prioritize your sessions and respect your time. If you are running late, reach out to your mentee as soon as possible to let them know. If you have to reschedule, do so as far in advance as possible so your mentee has time to reengineer their schedule and find a new time to get together.

- **Let key people know that you're participating:** HR should inform your supervisor that you are participating in the reverse mentoring program and make it clear that you will need to prioritize these sessions with your mentee. But you are responsible for letting your boss and your team know when you schedule meetings so they don't inadvertently schedule something else for those times, question your absence, or try to reach you when you're not available. If you need to be available at certain times of the day, work that out with your supervisor and your mentee before your first session. If you have an assistant or anyone else who reports to you, let them know when you'll be unavailable and why.

- **Don't rush to meetings:** The conversations you have with your mentee will likely at times be heavy and emotional. It's important to ensure that you're in the right headspace before engaging in these types of conversations. If you're distracted or stressed, you won't be fully present, so try to schedule at least a few minutes in advance of the meeting to refresh and prepare yourself mentally. Go to the bathroom, grab some water or a coffee, take a short walk outside, meditate—whatever helps you feel centered and calm.

- **Get to know one another:** Prior to your first official meeting, HR should reach out to both you and your mentee to schedule a short introductory session. This need not be longer than fifteen or twenty minutes and is basically designed to review the scope of the relationship so that everyone is on the same page about what is expected. After this initial introduction but before your first mentoring session, I recommend scheduling some one-on-one time with your mentee directly so you can get acquainted with one another before you begin the hard-hitting work of mentorship. Join them for lunch or coffee someplace where you can both feel at ease and focus on each other. There should be no agenda for this meeting other than learning more about one another's lives and pivotal experiences. Go beyond your basic résumé, career highlights, or job-interview talking points to share the formative experiences that made you who you are today. How did you end up in this career? What experiences helped shape your perspective on the world? What was your childhood like and how has that affected your life as an adult? Use these stories as an invitation to your mentee to share their own experiences, and follow up on the stories that pique your interest. Even though you're serving as the official mentor, you will no doubt learn a lot, too, by spending time with someone in your mentee's position. Stay curious and have fun.

CONDUCTING A MEETING

Before you delve into these intimate learning sessions, you'll want to set some ground rules for confidentiality, privacy, protocol, and communication. Be sure not to skip this step, as it will provide the foundation for a safe, productive relationship and ensure that there is no ambiguity surrounding your expectations of one another.

Once you've laid this foundation, you should be ready to start facilitating mentoring conversations. Ideally, these conversations will flow naturally, and you and your mentee will develop a rapport that allows each of you to share personal stories, perspectives, and experiences in a way that helps build empathy and understanding while keeping the primary goal of these sessions—to deepen your mentee's views on diversity, equity, and inclusion with an eye toward improving your organization—top of mind.

There are a few things you as a mentor can do to facilitate these conversations, techniques that allow for vulnerability without letting emotions become overwhelming.

Set the Tone

Because you, as the mentor, have more insight into the DEI issues that affect the group(s) with which you are affiliated, it is your role to hold the space for the mentee as you answer their questions. Your mentee will likely come to your meetings with a sense of what they want to focus on and where their gaps lie, and you should have a good sense of their overall goals after speaking with HR and attending the introductory meeting. But your mentee may not know what they don't know. If you feel that there are more relevant things to discuss than what they're suggesting, feel free to steer the conversation in a different direction. Here are some topics to consider:

- What policies and/or procedures at your organization affect certain groups differently than others?
- What barriers prevent certain people at your organization from succeeding?
- How are certain groups misrepresented or not represented at all?
- What was a specific moment at your company where you felt that your difference played a role in how you were perceived? How did it make you feel?
- What is an example of a time the organization missed an opportunity to address the needs of a particular group? What do you think that they could have done differently?

Be challenging with your questions. After all, your mentee is there to learn and make a difference.

Be Prepared

Your mentee may ask for some more information or follow up with you after a session to ask additional questions about a subject you discussed. You may decide to respond prior to the next session or wait until you can meet in person to continue the conversation. Regardless, be sure to set aside the necessary time to formulate a considered response and/or complete any necessary research. This demonstrates that you are committed to helping your mentee learn and prevents you from having to waste precious time in a session doing something you could have done more efficiently beforehand. In addition, if there is a specific issue or area of the company where you would like to see a change, come armed with the facts so that you are able to make a constructive argument.

Respect Your Mentee's Privacy

Your mentee will likely share things about their life or the organization that you should not repeat outside the meeting. They might also make themselves vulnerable to you by admitting past mistakes or revealing problematic behaviors or beliefs they are trying to change. In order for your mentee to get the most out of this experience, they need to open themselves up to learning and changing, and in order to do that, they must feel safe making themselves vulnerable with you. In Chapter 6, I will offer advice for you and your mentee to determine what information should and should not be shared and how to communicate that information outside of your private sessions. But, generally speaking, keep these conversations private unless given express permission to do otherwise. If your mentee shares something that makes you uncomfortable and you feel that it needs to be addressed, discuss it with your HR point person.

Keep an Open Mind and Refrain from Judgment

By signing up to participate, your mentee is acknowledging that they have a lot to learn when it comes to DEI. Admitting ignorance is hard, especially for leaders who are expected to project confidence regardless of their circumstances. In order to maintain a productive learning environment, the mentee must feel safe offering their opinion, sharing their own stories, or asking questions without fear of judgment. Doing so allows them to be just as vulnerable, which strengthens your bond and makes it more likely that your lessons will sink in. Remember, your mentee is here to learn. Sharing a personal or embarrassing story is also their way of communicating what help they need.

Stick to Facts

When sharing certain stories from your life, you may become emotional. This is natural and acceptable, and you and your mentee will have developed an environment in which you feel comfortable and safe expressing these emotions without having to worry about what each other will think. Don't fear your emotions; in fact, they are often the

most powerful tool you have to build empathy and communicate what it feels like to live in your shoes.

That said, our feelings about an event do not necessarily reflect the reality of that event, especially when that
event involves someone else. We often assign motivation
to other people's behavior based on our own motivations,
insecurities, and past experiences. How many times have
you assumed that a friend was mad at you because they
hadn't called you back when, in reality, they were just
busy?

When telling a story—especially if it involves other
people at your organization—stick to the facts as much as
possible and try not to assume someone else's thoughts, beliefs, or motivations. If a colleague used an offensive term,
they may have been malicious or they may have been ignorant, but their motivation doesn't matter to your mentoring conversation.* What matters is that the comment made
you feel excluded and unwelcome at your place of work,
and that your mentee now understands how that term affects people at the organization.

As another example, let's say a highly qualified woman
you work with was up for a promotion that was awarded to
a man who, from what you understand, is less experienced.
Unless you have proof or insight into the hiring manager's
decision-making process, you can't say for certain that this

---

* Of course, if this person has a history of making these sorts of comments and has
been reprimanded for it before, it may constitute harassment, which is an issue to
take up with HR.

was an act of gender discrimination. However, you could point out that this manager has only appointed men to senior positions in their time at the company or describe other problematic, perhaps sexist, behaviors they've engaged in as a way to show a pattern. Let the facts speak for themselves and you will make your point while earning a reputation as a trustworthy, levelheaded messenger.

Using Third-Party Examples

When your colleagues discover that you're participating in reverse mentoring, they may share their own insights and stories with you in the hope that you will either directly relay them to your mentee or that you will use what they tell you to inform your own conversations during the meetings. These people may share similar identities or backgrounds to yours, or they may be trying to educate you on their perspective as a member of a different group. It is entirely up to you to decide what to do with this information. If they give you permission to share it, you may decide to bring it up with your mentee, but you should only do so if you feel comfortable speaking on the other person's behalf. The DEI leadership team at your organization chose you to be a mentor because of your own stories, not because you are expected to be an expert on DEI or a representative of everyone from a marginalized background. You are not obliged to speak for other people if you don't want to.

If you do decide to share third-party stories, it's important to remember that another person's story is just that—another person's story. You might lack important context to tell it fully. If you feel that your mentee would benefit from hearing it, check with the person who shared it to make sure that they're okay with you bringing it up. They might prefer to remain anonymous, keep it between the two of you, or tell it in their own words to the mentee directly. Respect their decision. If you do share it, stick to the facts and maintain the confidentiality of other parties involved unless you also have their permission to disclose. If this other person and your mentee are open to speaking to one another directly, you can offer to introduce them and effectively "pass the mic," thus relieving the burden from you and ensuring that your mentee hears the complete and accurate story. Giving the other person the opportunity to share their story has the added benefit of allowing them to express their feelings about it, which will deepen your mentee's understanding of the experience.

HOW TO HANDLE THINGS WHEN THEY GO WRONG

Because your mentee, by their own admission, still has a lot to learn about inclusion, it is possible that they may say or do something (hopefully inadvertently) that offends or upsets you. This can be extremely jarring, perhaps even triggering, but ideally you will feel empowered to call out and correct the behavior in real time. Remember, you are the authority, the teacher in this situation. Your job is to help your mentee learn and improve, and that often requires correcting errors.

It's usually safe to assume that by choosing to engage in a reverse mentoring program, your mentee wants to correct their biases, blind spots, and harmful beliefs and behaviors. Even if they do or say something unacceptable, your default reaction should be to assume positive intent. When we assume positive intent, we assume that someone's bad behavior or disrespectful action is not a result of malice, prejudice, or intent to harm, but rather a result of ignorance, emotion, or something perhaps outside their control. When we assume positive intent, we prepare ourselves to respond with patience and empathy instead of offense and judgment.

If such a moment occurs, the best thing to do is to pause the conversation, point out what your mentee said or did, explain why it was problematic, and create space for them to respond. If all goes as it should, your mentee should thank you for the feedback, apologize, promise to do better, and not repeat the mistake.

If they struggle to understand why what they did was wrong, use this as a teachable moment. Try to be patient and answer their questions as best as possible. If you're not sure about the answer, be honest but make a commitment to find out. Sometimes, when people question us, especially if they've just said something we found objectionable, we feel as though they're arguing with us and default to a place of defensiveness. But, in this case, your mentee's questions should be coming from a place of genuine curiosity and a desire to learn. It may take a few additional examples and a deep conversation for them to understand why something is offensive; after all, this isn't their lived experience and they are on a learning journey.

When Anna, a Black mentor in finance, explained to her mentee, Michael, a Latinx sales leader, that she felt as though her contributions at work were diminished more times than not, Michael dove into solution mode. He asked her to give some examples because he wanted to see how he could "coach" her to perhaps be more forthcoming and assertive when presenting her ideas. He had assumed that she wasn't. Remembering that Michael coaching Anna was outside the boundaries of the reverse mentoring relationship, and the fact that Michael had presumed that the responsibility for being diminished sat with Anna as opposed to it sitting with her team, peers, and leaders, Anna requested that Michael pause and listen. Michael was offended that she didn't want his advice; he only wanted to help, after all. The rest of the conversation was stilted as Anna didn't feel listened to and Michael didn't feel appreciated. They ended the session early and Michael then spoke to the reverse mentoring program lead to explain the situation. As Michael recounted the conversation, he realized his error. How could he have been so arrogant as to (a) assume that Anna needed his input and (b) switch to senior mode so quickly (this was only their second session)?

Michael requested a short catch-up with Anna that same week and apologized. In addition, Anna shared that when she was "assertive," she had previously received feedback that individuals thought she was actually being "aggressive." As a result, she had become hyperaware of how others interpreted her actions and so found herself stuck between bringing her whole authentic self to work and holding back for the fear that some people might view her attempts to stand up for herself as "too much" or hostile. As a Latinx male, Michael could understand where she was coming from. He shared how, early in his career, he had learned to tone down his passion after learning that some people mistook it for aggression.

Of course, it's not always so easy to respond quickly and calmly the way Anna did when something like this happens. You may still feel intimidated by your mentee's authority in your organization. You may be triggered and default to a stress response due to similar past experiences. Or, you may just struggle to articulate why exactly the behavior was problematic. Try to remember that this is a safe space. Your feelings are valid. If you can't correct your mentee in the moment, you can ask to take a break or bring it up after your session or at your next meeting once you've had time to decompress. If you still need help, reach out to HR for advice. The worst thing you can do is nothing, not simply because you forgo the opportunity to actively educate your mentee and potentially prevent them from doing the same thing to someone else, but also because not addressing a problem allows it to fester, potentially compromising your ability to share openly with your mentee going forward. Please don't let a moment that could be used to teach a valuable lesson turn into something that undermines all the other hard work you and your mentee are doing together.

Of course, if the conversation becomes consistently uncomfortable and, upon reflection, you feel that boundaries have been challenged, reach out to the program lead to discuss your concerns. Though the intention is to create an environment in which both parties feel free to discuss challenging topics without being judged or harmed, if that space no longer feels safe, you must address this before you can move on.

AFTER THE MEETINGS

If you're only meeting with your mentee once a month or once every few weeks, it's easy to forget what you've discussed or let questions or conversations you promise to revisit fall by the wayside. That's why it's important to take some time after each meeting to write down what you discussed and follow up on any items that require extra attention. Did you offer to share an article or another resource with your mentee? Send it as soon as possible, ideally within a few hours of your meeting, so it's fresh in their mind. Did your mentee ask you a question you weren't prepared to answer immediately? Take the time you need to formulate a response and share it using whatever method you and your mentee decided upon at your first meeting. You may choose to follow up via email, wait until the next meeting, or even schedule a short intermediary session to discuss.

You might also find that, after a session, you feel the need to clarify or expand on something previously discussed. If this is the case, follow up as soon as you're able so the conversation is still fresh in your mentee's mind. During one of my mentoring sessions with the CEO of Virgin Atlantic, he asked me a few questions that I attempted to answer in the moment. But, as I reflected on them later that night, I realized that I hadn't been as clear as I could have been. The next day, I sent him an email letting him know that I'd considered his questions more deeply and wanted to refine my answers. He appreciated my candor and commitment to the mentoring process and even shared my insights with the head of the program.

Between sessions, consider what subjects you might want to share at your next meeting and take the time to do any necessary preparation. Remember, it is the mentee's responsibility to scope the sessions so they are getting out of them what they need. If possible, share your suggested ideas with your mentee in advance as they might want time to prepare for the discussion on their own.

IN CLOSING

Think about the opportunity you have to be listened to and *really* heard. You have the opportunity to have a captive audience in the form of someone with significant influence within your organization. As you embark on the journey, think about how you would like to be remembered. As you define your end goal, reflect on what you can do to increase your impact, gather stories from others, and really grasp the opportunity to be the spokesperson to light a flame within the organization to make a change.

As a mentor you may want to consider what role you would like to play in future programs. The journey of change is a long one, and many mentors I have spoken to, whether their experience was good or bad, shared that they still wanted to contribute to the organization by continuing to participate in the program in some guise—either by mentoring future mentors or continuing to take the time to be a mentor themselves.

Remember, too, that the ability to share your story and influence other people at your organization can positively impact how you view yourself. Take it from other mentors:

> I felt empowered, that I had an important role to play in expanding the knowledge of the leaders in the organization.
>
> OLIVER, retail assistant,
> global technology brand

I felt as though I had a voice, and I was being listened to.

HAYLEY, buyer, international fashion house

The program was set up in such a way that I felt as though my conversations were safe and my feelings were validated.

AMATULLAH, clinical assistant,
global pharmaceutical company

I gained confidence in challenging my mentees as I got more experienced and more senior. I challenged them to look more deeply into their areas and come up with action plans on how to address disparities. This experience allowed me to a have a greater level of visibility than I would have had otherwise.

THOMAS, manager,
multinational utility company

One of the most endearing reflections that was shared with me was from Karl, a manager within the engineering industry who became a mentor after one of his peers encouraged him to. Karl was a reserved individual who didn't really enjoy putting his head above the parapet and drawing attention to himself. This was the first time he had engaged formally in a program, and although he was nervous and apprehensive at the start, after a few sessions, his personal confidence had increased significantly—so much so that he has volunteered to lead a session with the next cohort of mentors. "I am confident that as a result of my participation in this program, real change will happen," he told me. "My mentee is so enthusiastic about making a difference, I feel more engaged and am more optimistic about my future in this organization but more so for those that are going to come behind me!"

CHAPTER SIX

THE FIRST SESSION—AND BEYOND

B y now, the mentor and mentee should understand your respective responsibilities and have taken the time to get to know one another in an informal setting so you can start to build a rapport. With this foundation of safety and vulnerability set, both of you can begin the important work of mentoring.

Because their schedule is likely more complex, the mentee should take initiative to schedule the first official mentoring session. Although subsequent meetings can be shorter (I recommend around sixty minutes), you should set aside more time (at least ninety minutes) for the first official session in order to allow time for some logistical and planning conversations that you only need to have once.

Once you've settled on a time for the first session, I also recommend going ahead and scheduling each of the subsequent sessions so you have them in your calendars and don't have to scramble to find an hour every month (or however often you choose to meet). Of course, you can always reschedule if necessary (provided you give the other person plenty of advance notice), but planning in advance ensures that you're prioritizing the meetings and that you can select an ideal time rather than letting outside forces dictate when you can meet. As we discussed in the previous two chapters, you want to select a time in which you are less likely to be stressed, rushed, tired, or unfocused so you are better prepared for the deep, important conversations that will take place during these sessions.

If possible, try holding the meetings on-site in your offices in order to reduce travel time and distractions. Though it may be tempting to get away from the hub-bub of the office or to pick a more neutral setting like a coffee shop or restaurant, when you only have a limited amount of time, you want to maximize every minute you have to converse and minimize the interruptions that usually happen in public places. Try to pick a meeting room that is soundproof (or nearly so) and private, with no interior-facing windows. If this is not possible, then try to position yourselves to face away from such windows during your session. Even if people can't hear your conversations or are not intentionally trying to eavesdrop, they can detect a lot from body language or facial expressions. And, in my experience, colleagues can't help but get curious when they see a senior member of management meeting one-on-one with someone, especially a more junior person.

Do *not* schedule meetings in the mentee's office. Though it may be more convenient to have their mentor come to them, and an executive office may ensure privacy and comfort, having the meeting in a neutral setting will help mitigate the effects of the power dynamic that already exists between the mentor and mentee. Plus, a new setting should help the mentee transition from day-to-day tasks and business conversations toward a mindset that is conducive to listening, learning, and growth.

ESTABLISH YOUR STANDARDS AND PREFERENCES

In order to ensure an effective relationship, mentors and mentees need to clarify their preferences and expectations around communication and confidentiality before beginning any official mentoring conversations. Doing this up front will establish trust that each party will treat the other in a way that is acceptable to them and that respects their boundaries as an individual and fellow employee. Don't assume that just because you are comfortable with something, the other person will be, too.

Communication

Given the ease with which people can communicate these days and the professional nature of the mentoring relationship, it's important to set guidelines around how and when you communicate with one another between sessions. Ask one another the following questions:

- What is your preferred method of communication, email or phone? (Note that cell phones should only be used if they have been issued by the company and/ or as a means to communicate an urgent message, for example that you're running a few minutes late to a meeting.)
- When is it appropriate for me to contact you directly, and when should I go through your assistant? (For example, a mentee may ask their mentor to carbon-copy their assistant on all emails to ensure that they don't get lost in their inbox. Similarly, both parties may prefer that all scheduling issues be handled by their respective assistants.)
- Are you open to scheduling additional meetings if the need or desire arises?
- How do you want me to follow up regarding action items or ideas for future discussions? (For example, you may decide that the mentee will send out an email within twenty-four hours following a mentoring discussion to summarize action items and topics to discuss in the future and/or email the mentor three days prior to the upcoming session to set an agenda for discussion.)

Confidentiality

Reverse mentoring requires both parties, especially the mentor, to share deeply personal stories, details, and beliefs with a colleague. In order to create an environment in which people feel safe being vulnerable in this way, they must feel secure that the other person respects their privacy and won't share any information they prefer to keep private outside of the mentoring sessions. That said, the ultimate goal of reverse mentoring is to improve the organization by educating and empowering leaders to create change around diversity, equity, and inclusion and, ultimately, to foster an increased sense of belonging among employees from all backgrounds. Thus, the mentee must be able to take what they've learned and act on it, which will likely require them to share their ideas and insights with other members of the organization.

Generally speaking, the mentee should not disclose any personal information about the mentor without the latter's express permission. If a mentor is extremely comfortable sharing, they could offer to default to the opposite, letting the mentee know that they should feel free to share any details they think are relevant unless the mentor asks them to keep something specific private.

Prashant had been part of his organization, a large pharmaceutical company based in Michigan, for five years when he decided to join its reverse mentoring program. As the government affairs director, he was relatively senior in the organization, but he offered to take part as a mentor, not a mentee, because he thought that other members of the leadership team could learn important lessons about inclusion from his lived experiences. Despite being born and raised in the United States, as a person of South Asian heritage, Prashant had experienced his share of prejudice, discrimination, and overt racism throughout his life, and he had a unique perspective on the company's efforts to promote inclusion and belonging. He recognized that if he—someone with a lot of authority and clout within the organization—had faced challenges or felt excluded because of his minority status, chances are that less-privileged employees from similar backgrounds had experienced the same—or worse.

Prashant was assigned to work with the chief commercial officer. Upon beginning their mentoring sessions, Prashant decided to share two stories from his tenure at the company that he felt exemplified the sort of treatment he, as a person of color, might experience in the workplace. The first took place during one of Prashant's first meetings with his new team. Upon introducing himself, several of his colleagues, most of whom were white, struggled to pronounce his name. After several attempts to get it right, one of his peers asked Prashant if they could call him "Paul" because (at least for him) it was easier to pronounce. Prashant was taken aback by the suggestion, but heard an audible hum of relief around the table as other people started nodding in agreement. Still trying to make a good first impression with his new colleagues and worried about being branded as difficult, Prashant agreed, even though he was frustrated and disappointed that in this day and age others, especially senior leaders, chose not to make the effort to pronounce his name correctly. In addition, knowing that the business is international, he wondered whether they behaved this way with customers and suppliers. Since that day, he had introduced himself as "Paul," and when anyone asked why, he'd tell them that's just what he preferred to be called.

Prashant also shared how, as part of his job, he frequently met with counterparts from other organizations and government bodies to negotiate and network about issues that affected their industry. Typically, the only people who attended these meetings were those who shared similar titles and roles with Prashant, but upon Prashant assuming his position, the general counsel (GC) of the company asked to attend all of these meetings as well. Not only did inviting this additional person complicate the meetings and scheduling, but it also required Prashant to spend considerable time briefing his GC in advance to get him up to speed on all the relevant topics. Prashant felt that the GC's request to attend these meetings meant one of two things. One, the company didn't trust Prashant to handle the meetings on his own, even though he'd come to the role with considerable experience and had been recruited directly by the CEO. Two, the company worried that his peer group (which was 90 percent white and male) would not take Prashant as seriously as a white person.

In sharing these two experiences, Prashant made it clear that he was open to his mentee sharing the first one (about his name) in forums outside of their meetings because he believed that it reflected the sort of everyday exclusions people from underrepresented backgrounds often face. As representatives of a global organization with offices in several locations around the world, plus the impact that this behavior could have on clients and prospective clients, leaders needed to understand how even casual remarks could affect their peers negatively. Prashant also wanted his fellow employees of color to feel empowered to speak up if they experienced a similar microaggression.

As part of the quarterly DEI update with the rest of the leadership team, Prashant's mentee shared this story, and shortly after, another leader reached out to Prashant directly to apologize. It turned out that he had been present at that meeting and had not considered how disrespectful it was to ask a colleague to go by a different name because others couldn't be bothered to pronounce it properly. The leader also shared how hearing this story from Prashant's perspective forced him to acknowledge other microaggressive behaviors he'd engaged in over the years without even realizing he was being discriminatory.

However, Prashant did not feel comfortable letting the story about the general counsel go any further for fear of repercussions. Understanding this sensitivity, the mentee kept this information confidential but used it to become more of a sponsor for Prashant in rooms he wasn't in. The mentee began actively encouraging Prashant's solo participation in external events as a way to support his profile and better reflect his status and value at the organization.

The mentee should be judicious about what they want to share with outside parties and why. Can a point be made, insight be shared, or action be taken without referring back to the mentor at all? Why might it be helpful to share certain details of the mentor's story with a larger group, and how can the mentee do so in a way that respects their mentor's privacy? If unsure, talk to the mentor and see if you can find a solution together.

Similarly, the mentee will share information about their own lived experiences with their mentor. Because the mentor is responsible for education, not action, there should be few, if any, scenarios in which it's necessary for them to reveal these private conversations to a third party, save perhaps HR. If such a situation arises, talk to the mentee about what's appropriate.

Before you as the mentor or mentee share anything, it's also important to make sure that you're communicating it accurately. We often project our own beliefs and ideas onto other people's stories and interpret their lessons differently from the person who lived through the experience. When asking for permission to share something, take the time to clarify with your mentoring partner whether you've interpreted it correctly so you don't communicate the wrong message unintentionally. The following script, which imagines a particular scenario and borrows a page from the active listening practice we discussed in Chapter 4, might help:

> The story you just told me about your induction process is really interesting. If I'm understanding it correctly, when you asked whether there was a prayer room in the building, the trainer didn't answer your question but instead suggested that if you needed special adjustments to work, then you should have listed this in the "accessibility" form you filled out when you accepted the position. Not only did you feel dismissed, you were also embarrassed because this episode took place in front of several other people—all strangers—some of whom sniggered in response to the trainer's answer. You wondered if this was the type of place where you could feel welcome if your questions weren't answered and if an HR professional seemed to believe that your religion was a form of "disability." Is that accurate?

In addition to personal information, the mentee will likely also share insight into challenges the business is facing or strategic conversations happening at the highest levels of leadership. More than likely, the mentor will already be aware of some of these issues, especially ones around DEI, because they've been shared with the company or may be obvious.

For example, the mentee may share strategic plans regarding a new product range or location move and ask the mentor's view on the subject to help inform their decision. Wary of the limits of just one individual's opinion, the mentee may then make a formal and confidential request to a specific employee resource group to review those plans and offer recommendations before going forward. The mentor and mentee should clarify which, if any, information the mentor can share outside of these conversations.

KICKING OFF THE CONVERSATION

Once you've agreed to communication and confidentiality standards, you can transition to the mentoring work. The mentee should kick things off by explaining what they hope to learn, what DEI challenges the company is facing, and their own personal experience with diversity, equity, and inclusion and/or particular groups.

Because these sessions are designed to help the mentee learn, it is important that they have the chance to communicate what they hope to achieve throughout the course of the relationship and why this process is important to them. The mentee should speak as both an individual and as a leader. Why are they personally invested in this experience, and how do they hope it will help them make better decisions on behalf of the organization? Both parties should keep in mind, of course, that the mentee represents just one voice in an entire organization that may have a long way to go on its journey toward belonging and inclusion. These sessions are just one of the many steps that need to be taken, and the mentee cannot guarantee that any particular action or change will occur as a result of what they learn.

Here are some questions the mentee should consider asking themselves at this point:

- What are your assumptions when it comes to diversity, equity, and inclusion? About what subject(s) or group(s) do you feel ignorant?
- How much experience do you have interacting with members of the group(s) your mentor represents and what was the nature of those experiences? What about your experience as a leader? For example, does your social or family circle consist primarily of people from your same socioeconomic or cultural background? What about your leadership team? Do you tend to gravitate toward people who represent diverse experiences from your own or who typically share similar backgrounds to you?
- What assumptions do you have or have you had regarding the group(s) with which your mentor is affiliated, and how has that affected your decisions as a leader? For example, if you are a man and/or don't have children, you may lack a basic understanding of

the pressures on working mothers and have therefore overlooked their needs in hiring or promotion
decisions.

- What is the current status of DEI at your organization, and what challenges are you facing?

- What are some past mistakes you've made as a leader
regarding DEI, and how do you interpret the consequences of those mistakes? How do you think reverse
mentoring might help you avoid mistakes like this in
the future?

- What is a formative experience you've had that
changed the way you see members of marginalized
groups? When was a moment you recognized your
own privilege? For example, maybe as a young person,
you smoked marijuana even though it was illegal but
never got arrested or fined for it. Later, when you met
a person of color who was incarcerated for possess-
ing marijuana, you may have realized how the color of
your skin likely exempted you from the consequences
that, more than likely, would have prevented you from
achieving the career success you have. How did that
make you feel?

The mentee should use this time to be honest and vulnerable and put their mentor at ease so they are invited
to open themselves up to them. They should also address
the power dynamic at work by proactively committing

to embracing the role of student. The mentee might say
something like this:

> I want to assure you that I respect your time and I am in
> full listening mode. I am here to learn from you, so if I
> slip into my traditional role of giving advice or trying to
> correct you, please point it out so I can stop. I recognize
> that my position in our organization might make it dif-
> ficult at first for you to feel comfortable with me, but I
> am eager to hear anything and everything you feel com-
> pelled to share with me and to respect your privacy and
> boundaries in the process. I am also committed to us-
> ing the insights I gain in these sessions to make changes
> within our organization to help advance diversity, eq-
> uity, inclusion, and a culture of belonging. If at any point
> you feel that I am not living up to that commitment, I
> want you to hold me accountable.

The mentee should give the mentor the opportunity
to ask questions or clarify their objectives. Ensure that you
both understand why you're here and what you're trying
to accomplish before you dive into the actual mentoring
conversations. Pay particular attention to making sure
that the mentor is clear on your company's DEI goals and
the mentee's role in helping achieve those goals. Your HR
and leadership teams should have already communicated
most of this information to all employees, especially if the
data was collected via an employee survey. Still, it's worth

making sure that the mentor has the right information and also hears directly from the mentee about what they want to focus on. For example, if the organization's leadership team already has a healthy representation among women, the CEO might be focused on increasing ethnic and racial diversity, but the vice president of engineering at the same company may find the opposite to be true within his department—a solid amount of racial and ethnic diversity but a lack of female representation.

ASKING QUESTIONS

Once the mentee has explained their intentions, desires, and goals, you two can begin a mentoring dialogue. To start, give the mentor the opportunity to discuss anything weighing on their mind and/or respond to anything the mentee shared. For example, one mentor I spoke with revealed that, as a member of a minority group within the organization, they struggled to understand the "rules of the game"—the unofficial politicking and cultural norms that dictated interactions—and, as a consequence, felt that they had repeatedly been passed up for promotion. They wanted to convey this to their mentee as it really affected their feeling of belonging within the business and was a common feeling among people from marginalized groups who felt like they were being sidelined. This enabled a deeper conversation, which allowed the understanding of the root of the issue. This mentor was a leader within a boutique investment house that had been set up with only thirty people and had grown rapidly over the years to a workforce of 1,000. He acknowledged that the friendly and familial atmosphere the team had prided itself on since the early days might now, with a more diverse workforce, feel exclusive and ostracizing to people who didn't fit the typical mold.

If the mentor doesn't have anything in particular they'd like to share to get started, the mentee should now ask questions to help ignite the conversation. Ideally, these questions should prompt the mentor to talk about their lived experiences, as that is the quickest, surest way to start breaking down the walls that usually stand in the way of us empathizing with and understanding one another.

Think back to the introductory conversation you previously had. Did the mentor share any details or stories that the mentee would like to learn more about? Did anything bring up a particular emotion—for either of you? Was there anything one of you didn't fully understand? Anything in particular about your career journeys or experiences at the company? Referring back to these details shows that you paid attention to and took great interest in what the other shared, which will help them feel safe and confident in moving through the relationship.

Here are some sample questions you can either ask or use as a template to formulate your own—at the first session and throughout your mentoring relationship. In fact, the following questions are open-ended and will enhance any conversation:

- Can you talk me through the most consequential decisions you made, and how you arrived at those decisions, throughout your career?
- Can you describe some of the experiences you had growing up that you recognized were unique to someone from your background?
- What has your experience, as a member of your particular group, been like at this organization? How does that compare to your experience at previous organizations?
- What did you expect your experience to look like when you joined the organization, and how has that differed from reality?

As your mentoring partner speaks, pay attention to things that elicit a strong reaction from them and try to find out more about what might be causing those reactions. Acknowledge the reaction and try to understand it by asking questions like: "I sense talking about this subject is bringing up some strong emotions for you. Can you tell me what you're feeling right now? Can you tell me what is behind this feeling?"

Similarly, you may find yourself reacting strongly to a story the other party shares, which is usually a sign to try to learn more. Don't shy away from these emotions; they are a sign that you're engaged in the conversation, which means you're primed to learn. Do you find yourself getting defensive or angry in response to something your mentor shared? Notice that feeling and see if you can use it as a learning moment. Use the active listening skills discussed in Chapter 4 to follow up and gain more insight. For example, if the mentor, a Black person, says that they distrust all cops and the mentee comes from a family full of police officers, the mentee might feel their hackles rise at this comment. Instead of interpreting the comment as an attack, the mentee should acknowledge that they had a different experience and ask their mentor to explain where their lack of trust comes from. The mentee doesn't need to adopt the same opinion—that all cops are untrustworthy—just understand why the mentor feels differently and try to empathize with their experience instead of simply seeing the world through their own eyes.

Another way to kick off a mentoring session—no matter what stage of the process you're in—is to discuss current events and their effect on organizations and individuals. We've seen this a lot in the past few years, especially with the rise of movements like Black Lives Matter, Me Too, and Stop Asian Hate, as well as the issues that came to light with the shutdowns and financial struggles people had during the COVID-19 pandemic. Some of these, like Me Too and the COVID-19 response, prompted immediate conversations and interventions within the workforce as they dealt specifically with workplace-related issues. Others, like Black Lives Matter, have left leaders at many companies scratching their heads over how to respond because the issues involved tend to elicit strong responses from both supporters and detractors and, at least on the surface, have very little to do with the day-to-day affairs of most workplaces. But these movements have had a profound effect on employees, particularly but not exclusively those who identify with the groups they seek to represent. More broadly, they have sparked conversations around how society treats these minority groups, thus forcing even slow-to-change organizations to address them. And, as we've found, many organizations end up doing so clumsily, issuing public-facing statements in solidarity with a particular movement or group while failing to look inward to examine how their own actions and cultures promote exclusion and discrimination.

The mentee may be looking for guidance on how to use their power and authority to do better, and, depending on how their mentor identifies, they may be able to offer valuable insights the mentee can use to influence their decisions. To start this conversation, the mentee should bring up the issue, movement, or sociopolitical conversation they're interested in, summarize their current understanding of it, and ask their mentor to describe how they view the issue. The mentee should try to reserve judgment or decide next steps until they've heard and processed their mentor's perspective.

In the summer of 2021, millions of soccer fans across Europe tuned into the hugely popular European Football Championship (aka the Euro Cup) after it had been delayed the previous year due to the COVID-19 pandemic.

Sporting events are often exciting and fun, but they can also be very tribal—at times violent—and during this particular tournament, two things happened to highlight the deeply rooted racism that existed across the continent. First, the Hungarian team was fined and forced to play its matches behind closed doors after their fans repeatedly engaged in racist and homophobic behavior, creating an unsafe environment for other fans and the opposing team. Then, in the final match of the tournament, England lost to Italy in a penalty shootout, and three young Black players on the English team, Marcus Rashford, Jadon Sancho, and Bukayo Saka, immediately became the targets of intense, racist online abuse from irate fans. As if this weren't upsetting enough, some fans even targeted Black civilians, leading to a few weeks of heightened racial tension in the United Kingdom following the match. One mentor, Cyrus, a Black man working in finance at a bank, used this event as an opportunity to discuss his experiences with his mentee Jared, vice president of the operations team and a white man.

Both men had found a common love of football, and even though they generally rooted for different local teams, they were both rooting for England in the Euro Cup. After the final, they discussed the racist response to England's loss. "We talked about my experience and how this comes to life at work and how perhaps the color of my skin affects my view of the world," Cyrus later told me. "Over the past week, it has been disappointing but not surprising to see the increase in racism in the UK as a result of the three Black players missing the penalty in the final."

Jared agreed that the fans' behavior was appalling, but also deflected the issue of racism by pointing to the role social media platforms like Twitter and Facebook play in allowing such rhetoric. "I can't believe that in this day and age they allow these things to be posted."

Cyrus felt that Jared was missing the point and that the episode indicated something much larger at work in the culture. "This is what happens on a regular basis," he said. "This incident has just highlighted how prevalent it actually is and that in fact those online racists feel free and almost empowered to post as there have never been any repercussions for this form of online bullying." He also pointed to a certain hypocrisy and denial at work in the United Kingdom:

From 2020, when businesses and media fought to paint a picture of civilized Britain versus the "barbaric" USA [in the wake of George Floyd's murder], it was clear that there was denial that racism still existed in a wider form in the UK. This unfortunate event proved that indeed it is still very much alive and still very ugly. In my family's WhatsApp group, my aunts were asking us boys/men to stay inside and make sure we don't travel alone for fear of attack. All over a game of football. It reminded me, and those within my community, that there is conditional acceptance for us. If we perform at the same level as others and even deliver winning performances, then we are allowed to stay, are tolerated. However, if we underperform, then we are treated far worse than those who fit the norm.

Hearing Cyrus share his perspective and personal experiences as a Black man forced Jared to reckon with his own blind spots and commit to doing better. He thanked Cyrus for sharing and told him that he wanted to talk to the rest of his leadership team to make sure that they were providing the appropriate support to individuals who had been affected by this incident and who might feel unsafe. He also committed to thinking more deeply about how UK society had impacted his own viewpoints and to challenging others to do the same.

Ultimately, the mentor should walk away from every mentoring session feeling listened to and understood and with the sense that the mentee gained a valuable lesson that they will carry with them as long as they go on to make decisions. The more you practice these conversations, the easier they will be.

CHAPTER SEVEN

ACTING ON INSIGHTS

Now that your reverse mentoring program is underway, it's time to turn your attention toward what you plan to do with the information and insights you glean throughout this process. Remember, the purpose of reverse mentoring is more than just educating leaders or making them better people. It's also more than engendering empathy among individuals who might not appear to have much in common or to give voice to employees who have less formal power within your organization. Yes, these are all byproducts of a strong reverse mentoring program, but the ultimate goal is to *use what you learn to inspire and inform real change*. Unless you take real, concrete steps to address the issues you uncover through this program, as well as any other diversity, equity, and inclusion efforts you've undertaken, your organization will never improve and, most likely, the mentors who shared their stories will feel used and betrayed.

In this chapter, we will discuss how to transform the insights you've gained from your reverse mentoring program into actions that can help you achieve your larger DEI goals. The responsibility for doing this lies with whoever is overseeing the reverse mentoring program and DEI strategy at your organization. Because this will most likely be human resources, I will be referring to that department throughout, but the advice is meant for any individual or team involved.

GATHERING INFORMATION

Since reverse mentoring is part of your larger DEI roadmap and you've likely already identified areas where your organization requires improvement thanks to surveys and other feedback mechanisms, you will likely already be on the lookout for specific types of insights for a particular group. To give you an example, in one organization I have worked with, it was clear that Black individuals were severely underrepresented in mid-management levels, much less in senior positions. The associated employee resource group had reported some areas for improvement in the recruitment and policy of the business, but there was still something fundamentally wrong. HR and the leadership team wanted to understand from an individual perspective what the contributing factors to this might be.

Within your program, your mentors may also share stories or perspectives you didn't anticipate, so it's important that you come up with a formal way to track and follow up on feedback in order to ensure that you hear everyone and don't overlook vital information that may spell the difference between a successful program and a missed opportunity.

In Chapter 3, we discussed three key points at which HR should formally check in on the reverse mentoring participants: after the second official mentoring session, after the fourth session, and after the final session has been completed. It's possible, of course, that mentors or mentees may communicate feedback at other points during the relationship if they think they've uncovered something important or encountered an issue that requires further investigation or action.

Obviously, you should always take immediate action if you discover something that is actively making your workplace unsafe for employees. For example, if a mentor shares that another employee has a history of bullying, intimidation, harassment, or other problematic behavior, you'll want to follow whatever procedure HR has in place to address this behavior as soon as possible and ensure that it isn't part of a larger trend within the organization.

Regarding less urgent matters, you may decide to immediately act on feedback if it could benefit any existing DEI initiatives. For example, if your team is currently auditing your company's benefits and a mentor shares how a benefit offered by a previous employer helped them tremendously—for example, a mental health program or a medical benefit that addresses the needs of a particular group—you might take that into consideration when researching any new benefit packages for the coming year.

Once a reverse mentoring cycle has ended, you'll want to gather all of the feedback from mentors and mentees and assess areas that require more attention. For example, I have introduced a comprehensive survey that is sent to the mentor, mentee, and program coordinator, which is then reviewed holistically to understand whether there are any key themes that are prevalent. For example, is there a particular team or level within the organization where people from certain groups experience discrimination? Is there a process or policy that has contributed toward inequity? Having a wide range of mentors and mentees will help to distinguish whether issues are isolated or more entrenched within the organization.

Here are some additional actions to take and questions to ask to solicit feedback:

- Encourage your mentors and mentees to share their thoughts on new and existing company policies and procedures as part of their conversations with one another.
- Has the mentor taken advantage of a new policy or benefit designed to address inequities?
- Have they found it useful?

- Have there been any unintended consequences, positive or negative?
- How has a new policy affected the mentee's leadership style?
- How has it impacted their team or their outlook on the organization?

NEXT STEPS

Although the ultimate actions you take will depend on the particular issues at hand and your unique needs as an organization, there are, broadly speaking, four groups who should be working to dig deeper and implement meaningful changes, depending on what they are: human resources, the leadership team, employee resource groups, and external experts.

Human Resources

If you receive feedback that there are issues with a domain that HR usually oversees (policies, talent, reward, and well-being), you'll need to address these directly with the rest of the HR team.

Consider Policy and Process

Is there an underlying culture within a department or across the business that is making certain groups feel uncomfortable or unsafe? Is there an underlying bias with your onboarding process or training? Do employees from certain groups feel uncomfortable talking to people in HR, due to lack of understanding or confidentiality?

Consider Business Norms

Are there standard practices or cultural norms at your organization that may be excluding certain groups? For example, do you frequently host social or networking events at bars or other establishments where the primary activity is the purchase and consumption of alcohol? If this is the case, colleagues from certain religions, struggling with addiction, or managing an illness that makes drinking dangerous may not join in these activities. As a result, others may assume that they are antisocial or not interested in engaging with colleagues, which may hurt their chances of establishing the professional relationships that can help them prosper in their careers. In addition, if social events are always in the evening, then it can make it very difficult for those individuals with caregiving responsibilities to attend, relax, and network as others would be able to. Both of the above examples were mentioned in a reverse mentoring relationship I helped facilitate and then taken to the relevant ERG for further discussion. It turned out that the respective ERGs had voiced these concerns before to little reception. In this way reverse mentoring acted as a calibration point for both HR and leaders within the business to listen intentionally to underlying issues that had been ruminating for a while.

If you come across incidences that suggest that policy, process, or business norms may be contributing to inequity, you may need to do a self-audit of your department to determine what, if anything, you can improve. For example, when you observe the data that you have—joiners, leavers, promotions, complaints, grievances raised, plus results of any employee surveys, which can give additional insight— is there a pattern that you can identify? Consider what the potential root causes of these issues could be. Oftentimes, we look at instances in isolation; when we do this, we fail to pick up patterns, but a self-audit is a great way to start painting the big picture.

The Leadership Team

If an issue is directly attributable to your leadership team, then HR will have to work directly with them to assess it and, if serious, decide on any actions that need to be taken. For example, if the leadership team's succession plan doesn't feature diversity (that is, it is a replication of the current team), then they will need to commit to diversifying their pipeline and create a plan (in consultation with HR) to hire, sponsor, and promote more individuals from diverse backgrounds. This may include setting diversity targets or connecting performance bonuses to meeting certain DEI goals, as with other key strategic commitments. Are your leaders aware of the following?

- Distinct representation gaps
- Their role in creating or upholding these gaps
- Where they are as an organization versus their competition or best in class
- Where they need to be, what change they are committed to, and what they need to do to get there

Employee Resource Groups

ERGs are a relatively recent phenomenon; some consider them to be affinity groups for support, providing a level of tacit reverse mentoring for allies. Others consider them a business resource group, an important stakeholder for policy and strategy. Overall, they are communities within organizations that provide a safe space for underrepresented employees and their allies to have conversations and share viewpoints. When the power of these groups is harnessed correctly, they have the potential to offer the organization a great deal of insight.

For the purposes of this section, we will assume that you have established ERGs in your organization. If your organization currently lacks an ERG to address the needs of a specific group, then HR should oversee this process by bringing people from shared backgrounds together as a focus group. If you choose to do so, ensure that participants are sufficiently briefed and that there is a high level of psychological safety prior to embarking on these sessions. If you determine that there is enough need and interest, you could even consider setting up a new ERG as part of your action plan. Studies show that ERGs support underrepresented groups and help foster a sense of inclusion and belonging within an organization. Most importantly, they provide these groups with a collective voice, which is more powerful than an individual one.

In many cases, a particular insight from a reverse mentoring program might require more information, analysis, or assessment from the impacted group in order to determine appropriate action. Though a mentor may offer specific recommendations they feel would help further DEI at the company, and those recommendations might seem reasonable, you'll want to give others who will be affected the chance to weigh in before making any decisions. Employee resource groups are a great tool for this.

Chances are that many of your mentors—especially early on in your program—will belong to one or more ERGs because their membership indicates a willingness to do this kind of DEI work. If this is the case, they can easily convey knowledge both to and from the group. In Chapter 5, we discussed how mentors may use their perspective as ERG members to inform discussions with their mentee, but the reverse is also true. Human resources, working alongside mentors, should also make sure to communicate any insights gleaned as part of reverse mentoring with the appropriate ERG if they feel follow-up is necessary.

As part of this stage in the program, you should consult an ERG if (a) you want to corroborate information shared during the program to see if other members of the group represented by the ERG share similar experiences or perspectives and (b) you need help determining which, if any, actions you should take to address a specific issue.

For example, if a mentor who is a working mother shares that her schedule makes it difficult to spend time with her children during the week and the company employs a lot of working parents, you may work with your caregivers ERG to understand more about the issues other caregivers are facing. You can then use the insight from this group to explore what changes you might be able to make to better accommodate your colleagues:

- Can you institute a flexible working policy?
- Could you implement custom schedules that better fit with the school day?
- Is it possible to provide an on-site childcare program?

Not only will your ERGs have opinions on what will be most helpful for them, but they can also offer suggestions you may not otherwise think of.

External Experts

In some cases, your internal groups may lack the know-how or resources to determine the best course of action, in which case you should consider hiring outside experts. Although doing so will require some additional expenditure, hiring them saves time and demonstrates your commitment to making meaningful change happen more quickly than you could otherwise do alone. Not only do external experts and consultants have the knowledge, resources, and tools you might lack, but they also have recent and more extensive experience working with other organizations and can share those insights when helping you figure out the best course of action. For example:

- What is the latest best practice when it comes to supporting ERGs (process, finances, structure, governance, and so on)?
- How should an organization with your structure set up and manage successful reverse and/or traditional mentoring programs?
- What is the latest thinking in managing diversity?
- What do you need to consider with regard to inclusion in a multi-generational workforce?

A company I worked with had already set up a successful reverse mentoring program spearheaded by a very strong lead from the business's ethnicity network. They sought mentors from the network who were not self-interested and paired them with the willing mentees. Although this initiative was not founded with HR, it quickly grew in popularity and the organization expressed interest in expanding the program. The lead could not commit the time to matching and managing the programs on such a large scale, so I was enlisted as an external consultant to audit the already existing programs and support the larger rollout.

COMMUNICATING INSIGHTS

Once you've shared your insights with the appropriate people and have worked with them to determine which actions to take, you'll want to communicate those changes to the rest of the organization. In Chapters 3 and 4, we discussed how HR and mentees in leadership positions should share results about their reverse mentoring experiences as part of regular communications with their teams and the organization as a whole. Though at first these communications may mostly consist of the participants' personal experiences and metrics about the program itself, as you move forward, you'll want to incorporate the broader actions you are taking as a direct result of the program.

Too often we hear leaders talk about how they've "listened" or have "realized their own biases" but then stop short of actually doing the things required to make a difference. Listening, building empathy, educating oneself, recognizing one's privilege—all of these things are crucial to dismantling the oppressive systems and attitudes that have held people from marginalized groups back for so long. But they are not enough. True leadership requires allyship, and true allyship often requires sacrifice.

However, what we mostly see from companies is performative allyship, public displays of solidarity, or declarations of support backed up by little or no real commitment to doing the work that needs to be done to actually improve the lives of people from underrepresented groups.

Case in point, in 2020, just a few months after George Floyd's murder, I was approached by a large, international brand to help them implement a more robust DEI strategy. As part of this strategy, they decided to establish an ethnic minority network to provide a safe space for ethnic minorities and allies to meet and support each other, as well as provide a collective voice to the business at large. The employees (mostly Black) who had volunteered to set up the initiative had been working for several months to secure sponsorship but had been met with delays and setbacks because they weren't receiving the support they needed from the leadership team. Then, midway through October (which is Black History Month in the United Kingdom), the CEO, who had failed to respond to most of the team's requests to that point, reached out to ask whether the network had been set up. When he learned that the team had been struggling, he informed them that they must set up the network before the end of the month. The team scrambled to meet the new deadline, and even though they were successful, the experience left them feeling disempowered and bitter that the company was only willing to pay attention to their needs when it was convenient, a quintessential performative action.

That same year, a new term—"wokefishing"—took hold of Internet discourse to describe people—and companies—who pretend to care deeply about diversity, equity, and inclusion in an effort to attract others but whose actions suggest otherwise. One American acquaintance of mine told me an extremely disheartening story of wokefishing at her company. Amid the Black Lives Matter protests of 2020, several members of the leadership team asked to discuss the company's response during one of their regularly scheduled strategy meetings. They hoped to issue a statement in support of the movement and develop an initiative that could help address equality gaps among both employees and clients. They assumed that the CEO, a white man who had received national and international praise for his progressive workplace policies, would be on board and give them the okay to move forward. Instead, the CEO quickly became agitated and accused the other leaders of wasting his time. He spoke about how important the cause was to him and bragged vaguely about all of the work he'd been doing outside of the office to support the protestors. He chastised senior managers who challenged him, but offered no ideas or solutions to the issue at hand. At one point he explained how racism worked to a senior manager—a white woman who had long worked to make the company more inclusive and had a reputation for taking the time to fully understand the experiences of people from different backgrounds. Employees left the meetings feeling belittled, disillusioned, and disempowered. Although they eventually decided to create a task force to focus exclusively on DEI issues, much of the momentum and passion the team had had for the cause had evaporated once they realized that they lacked full institutional support—and that their supposedly "woke" CEO was more interested in making people think that he was an ally than acknowledge that he and the company had a lot of work to do.

Emphasizing the actions you're taking as part of your regular DEI communications not only helps spread awareness of those actions so your employees can see that you're committed to improvement, but also holds you accountable to following through on those actions and forces you to get specific about your goals and plans for achieving them.

To create a robust communication plan, there are several key components to include:

- **The organization's overall DEI goals:** Have you committed to hiring or promoting a certain number of individuals from a specific background by a specific date? Are you looking to improve your metrics for inclusion and belonging? If you've already laid out your DEI goals in a previous communication, continue to remind people of what they are so they understand the context for the steps you're taking.
- **The status of the mentoring program:** How many people are participating in this cohort, and (if this is not the first mentoring cycle) how many total have

participated so far? Who are the current participants and what roles are they playing? What selection criteria did you use and/or what areas are you focusing on with this cohort?

- **Takeaways from previous cohorts:** What insights did you gain from the most recent program regarding DEI at your organization? How did participants respond to the program? What, if anything, surprised you? How do these takeaways compare to previous takeaways (either from previous mentoring sessions or other DEI surveys or initiatives)?

- **Next steps:** What are you planning to do with this information? Is there additional analysis you're doing? Are you planning to discuss it with particular groups? What, if any, action steps have you decided to take in response?

- **Future deadlines:** When do you expect to have completed the next steps that you listed?

A good example of this type of communication can be found in Deloitte's "Black Action Plan," an initiative the firm launched in the wake of George Floyd's murder to increase Black representation within the organization and address the specific needs of Deloitte's Black employees, of its clients, and in society at large.* The plan highlights five commitments the firm has made to achieve this goal:

---

* Deloitte UK, "Black Action Plan," accessed November 29, 2021, https://www2 .deloitte.com/uk/en/pages/about-deloitte-uk/articles/black-action-plan.html.

1. "We will provide equal opportunities."
2. "We will focus on developing people to succeed and thrive."
3. "We will drive and evolve our culture and behaviors."
4. "We will leverage the Deloitte brand and platform."
5. "We will measure and report on the targets and outcomes."

Although these commitments are extremely broad, each section of the report highlights specific actions the company took over the previous year to address each one, as well as their plans for continued action the following year. For example, as part of their commitment to "measure and report on the targets and outcomes," they stated their goal of having 12 percent of their partners represent ethnic minorities and 3 percent be Black by 2025, and they shared the results of their most recent round of promotions and its impact on their overall goal.

WHEN TO COMMUNICATE EXTERNALLY

Public displays of allyship mean nothing if they are not backed up by real change. Though it may seem like good PR—even an act of accountability—to announce your plans and commitments to the world, it's best to wait until you have taken real action before publicly announcing anything. By focusing first on your employees, you demonstrate that your commitment is to the organization, not to outside perception of the organization. When employees perceive this commitment, they trust the organization and its leaders more, which makes for a stronger, more inclusive culture.

Once you have done the work internally and you feel that the insights are worthy of sharing, you may choose to communicate your efforts externally. Though doing so can certainly help elevate your brand (when backed up by action), there are several other reasons to share your work with the world that go well beyond the profit motive and can actually help inspire change beyond the capacity of your organization.

From my research I have found that the tipping point is where you feel you've done enough work internally to warrant an external announcement. And that means that your reverse mentoring program is authentically and credibly working internally, not just to have those "aha moments" with the leaders so they can realize their privilege. What you really need is for your organization to take tangible actions with a clear and robust roadmap to building diversity and inclusion. By being brave and concrete about your aspirations, as an organization, you are willing to be held accountable. Here is what you should hope to achieve by sharing information publicly:

- **Spreading awareness:** Because your data is unique to your organization, you may be able to use it to tell a unique story that might inspire others to look deeper. For example, by sharing how your reverse mentoring program allowed your organization to uncover a blind spot it didn't know existed, you might inspire others to think differently about their own approach to DEI.

- **Offering advice:** If you implement a policy or procedure that helps improve your DEI metrics, you're contributing to the body of research that allows other organizations to make informed decisions about their own initiatives. Consider, for example, how Jack Welch first used reverse mentoring at General Electric to help educate his older staff members on new technologies and how that strategy has since been used to profound effect at other organizations all over the world.

- **Aiding in attraction and retention:** By publicly sharing your commitment to diversity, equity, and inclusion, you make your brand more attractive to potential customers *and* employees. Widening your talent pool increases your chances for hiring the right people and enhancing the diversity in your ranks to improve decision-making and performance. It also demonstrates your commitment to supporting and listening to employees from marginalized groups; they are more likely to contribute to future initiatives—and will certainly do their best work—when they feel included. It's a win-win.

COMMIT TO CONTINUOUS IMPROVEMENT

No single action you take—no matter how impactful or effective—will solve all of your DEI concerns at once, and no matter how committed you are to creating an organization that fully embraces and values all of its people, you will never get it exactly right. But that's okay. The drive for more diversity, equity, and inclusion is not a quest for perfection; it's a journey of continuous learning and improvement, an ongoing process that requires dedication and more than a little dose of humility to recognize where you have fallen short, and where you have room to grow.

In order for an organization to be successful over the long term, it must learn how to adapt along with its community. In other words, as society changes, you must change, too. As such, for those who work in the DEI space, it can often feel like the goalposts are always shifting; the minute you seem to have solved one problem, you become aware of another issue or someone points out an error you made that requires immediate attention. It's like that classic arcade game of Whac-A-Mole, except instead of trying to tap toy groundhogs with a mallet, you're trying to make decisions that fundamentally affect people's lives.

Take language. Not too long ago, people of African descent in the United States preferred the term "African American" to identify their race. But in the past few years, Black, with a capital B, has gained wider acceptance because it more accurately describes non-Americans or people from

Afro-Caribbean cultures. Similarly, those in the LGBTQ+ community have fully embraced the once-pejorative term "queer" in addition to previously accepted terms like "gay," "lesbian," or "homosexual" because the former more broadly describes the full spectrum of sexual identities. In both cases, people who had previously been conditioned to think of terms like "Black" and "queer" as derogatory are now having to unlearn what they'd been taught and accept that their old ways of thinking are outdated.

If you're going to create an organization that fully represents and supports all of its people, you need to stay open to feedback, criticism, and new information and to commit to continuous learning and improvement. This means not only implementing changes but also monitoring the impact of those changes while consistently being on the lookout for other opportunities to grow.

As management guru Peter Drucker famously said, "If you can't measure it, you can't improve it." How you measure your progress will depend on the nature of whatever programs, policies, or procedures you put in place as well as your needs and goals as an organization. As a general rule, include a feedback mechanism as part of any new initiative, and monitor participation and engagement with new programs or resources. Refer back to the DEI goals and metrics you established in Chapter 2 to assess how your latest efforts move you closer to (or further away from) them.

Of course, numbers and surveys don't tell the full story. Organizations welcome data because it's relatively easy to understand. A 12 percent increase in promotions of people from diverse backgrounds is better than a 5 percent increase. A higher positive response rate to an employee engagement survey is better than a lower one. And so forth. But these metrics can only go so far in measuring a person's experience—how they feel about working at your organization and how their experience compares to those of others.

In fact, when companies rely on an overly data-driven approach to measuring progress, it can actually deemphasize the very things that make for a more inclusive and welcoming organization. These are things like connection, empathy, respect, and an overall sense of belonging. In order to measure these things, you need to take a more human approach, one that centers the experience of the individual and uses the power of storytelling to communicate information that can then be considered when making decisions.*

Fortunately, you already have a mechanism in place for this kind of humanistic feedback: your reverse mentoring program. As more and more people participate in your program, and as you continue to use the insights gained from these sessions to enact real change to address concerns among underrepresented groups, you will find that these twin initiatives start to work together organically as a type

---

* Selena Rezvani and Stacey A. Gordon, "How Sharing Our Stories Builds Inclusion," *Harvard Business Review*, November 1, 2021, https://hbr.org/2021/11/how-sharing-our-stories-builds-inclusion.

of feedback loop. New reverse mentoring participants will come to the table prepared not only with their personal experiences and perspectives but also with the awareness of what your organization has done to address the needs and concerns of those who came before them.

Since the summer of 2020, a plethora of organizations have launched reverse mentoring programs as a way to demonstrate that they are willing to listen. However, though there is a great deal of information about the launch of these programs, there is very little that details the completion of committed actions and the meaningful change made. Everyone can sniff out inauthenticity: when either or neither of the internal or external messaging really reflects the reality of what is actually happening in the organization. What will you do to demonstrate your commitment to rebalancing the scales of equity?

CHAPTER EIGHT

THE JOURNEY FORWARD

Throughout this book, I've spoken about how reverse mentoring can help your organization achieve more diversity, equity, and inclusion by allowing individuals from different backgrounds to learn and grow from one another. When we connect with other human beings through intimacy and vulnerability and really take the time to appreciate how their identities have shaped their lived experiences in ways that are different from our own, we change. We naturally gain deeper empathy and awareness and start to pay greater attention to how our actions—and the actions of others—affect the lives of those around us. We start to behave differently. To think differently. To speak differently. Even to feel differently. We begin to change because we have no other choice; refusing to do so—to deny what we have learned—would be to deny our own humanity and turn a blind eye to the needs and desires of others.

When people change, institutions change. And when institutions change, society changes. This is called progress, and it's a fundamental part of the human condition. What separates us from all other living beings is our ability to innovate—to imagine a different way of doing things and to turn those ideas into actions.

In the past few decades, we've already seen a lot of innovation when it comes to the subjects of diversity, equity, and inclusion. Up through much of the 1990s, most organizations who focused on these issues really only focused on one aspect: diversity. But as time went on and companies started becoming more diverse—thanks to specific programs and initiatives as well as natural shifts in the demographics of the labor force—we realized that simply hiring or promoting people from different backgrounds did not create the types of anti-discriminatory cultures we were striving for. As such, we began to recognize the need for inclusion—a culture in which people from diverse backgrounds are not just present but actively invited to participate, offer ideas, and make decisions.* More recently, we've begun to appreciate the need for equity, in other words programs and policies that level the playing field so that

---

* Robin J. Ely and David A. Thomas, "Getting Serious About Diversity: Enough Already with the Business Case," *Harvard Business Review*, November–December 2020, 6, https://hbr.org/2020/11/getting-serious-about-diversity-enough-already-with-the-business-case.

all members of an organization have an equal chance to succeed and thrive.

You cannot create a culture where everyone feels valued, respected, and safe without diversity, equity, and inclusion, but these things, in and of themselves, are not the goal of our efforts toward progress. Rather, they are building blocks to something much deeper, more fundamental, and more powerful. The goal of these efforts is not simply that everyone feels represented, included, and treated fairly. The goal is to create a culture in which everyone in your organization feels a deep sense of purpose, pride, and acceptance—because, not in spite, of the traits and attributes that make them who they are. In a word, we are striving toward belonging.

THE QUEST FOR BELONGING

Humans are innately social creatures. We crave connection with others and can readily sense when we're being included in or excluded from a situation or a group. Whenever we enter into a novel situation with people we don't know—whether it's a party filled with strangers, a new neighborhood, or a new job—we immediately pick up on social cues that tell us whether or not we're welcome. A friendly smile or an invitation to come join the conversation can make us feel at ease, while a mocking comment or an icy stare can trigger us to want to head for the hills.

Ultimately, we all crave a sense of belonging, the feeling we get when we are comfortable being who we are without fear of reprisal or judgment. When we feel like we belong, we become alive. Instead of worrying about what others think about us or our actions, we can focus on doing what we were put on this earth to do. Like a tree planted in fertile soil in a habitable climate, we flourish and grow, drawing on the energy around us to reach our full potential.

By contrast, when we feel excluded, we spend this energy worrying about the consequences of being singled out. This is a holdover from our most ancient history, a time when human beings literally depended on one another for survival and those who were ostracized from the clan were left to fend for themselves, alone in the wilderness without shelter, sustenance, or support.

Though the consequences may not be as bleak today, at a basic, unconscious level, we still perceive exclusion as a life-or-death threat and therefore often respond based on our instincts for self-preservation. We either shut down, thinking that we can protect ourselves from further harm by not attracting any unnecessary attention, or we pretend to be someone we're not in an effort to fit in or curry favor. Either way, we prevent ourselves from thriving because we are denying our true identities and needs and expending enormous amounts of energy trying to gain acceptance and approval instead of using it to create the lives we want. Imagine an oak tree planted in a desert, searching in vain for a place to put down roots in the dry, unstable sand beneath it. Instead of growing into a welcome source of shade, sustenance, and shelter, it shrivels up, unable to participate in the ecosystem around it.

As an organization, you want to create an environment that allows your people to grow and thrive, not one that chokes them off at the root. To do this, you need to foster a culture of belonging, one that allows all individuals—regardless of their backgrounds or experiences—to feel welcome and accepted for who they are and what they do. Research shows that when employees feel a strong sense of belonging at work, they are six times more likely to be engaged in their jobs than those who don't.[*] They are half as likely to leave the company, perform at 56 percent higher capacity, take 75 percent fewer sick days, and are more willing to recommend their employer to others than those who feel like they don't belong.[†]

By contrast, people who feel excluded are more likely to feel alienated and burnt out and to underperform than their peers.[‡] One study found that even a single instance of a "micro-exclusion"[§] can cause an immediate 25 percent

---

[*] Archana Ramesh, "Why Belonging Is Important at Work: Employee Engagement and Diversity," Glint, April 23, 2020, https://www.glintinc.com/blog/why-belonging-is-important-at-work-employee-engagement-and-diversity/.

[†] BetterUp, "The Value of Belonging at Work: New Frontiers for Inclusion," accessed November 16, 2021, https://f.hubspotusercontent40.net/hubfs/9253440/Asset%20PDFs/Promotions_Assets_Reports/BetterUp_BelongingReport_121720.pdf, 4.

[‡] Tomas Chamorro-Premuzic and Katarina Berg, "Fostering a Culture of Belonging in the Hybrid Workplace," *Harvard Business Review*, August 3, 2021, https://hbr.org/2021/08/fostering-a-culture-of-belonging-in-the-hybrid-workplace.

[§] BetterUp, "Value of Belonging," 11.

drop in an individual's performance.* As one person de-scribed it: "The office banter and socials were so cliquey, after a few months I stopped going. I always found excuses as I felt uncomfortable. It has been two years now. I always thought I would join at some point, but they stopped invit-ing me and now, well, I feel excluded."

These statistics shouldn't come as a surprise because we all know how dramatically different we feel when included versus excluded. Imagine that a friend invites you to a party where you don't know anyone. You walk into this strange room, surrounded by people you don't know, but, for your friend's sake, you decide to make the most of the evening. You overhear a group of people chatting amiably about a topic that interests you, so you decide to join in. You in-troduce yourself and mention your interest in the topic, and the strangers immediately introduce themselves and ask for your thoughts. You share them, they listen intently, and before long you're deep into a lively conversation with people who clearly value and enjoy your company. You re-lax, feel engaged, and have a great time.

Now imagine that you walk over to the same group of people and they respond completely differently. They be-have as though you've interrupted them and dismiss your contributions. They turn their backs toward you and cut you off when you try to speak. Instead of lighting up, you skulk in a corner, afraid to introduce yourself to anyone

---

* BetterUp, "Value of Belonging," 5.

else or speak up too loudly for fear of another rejection. As a result, the room does not benefit from your contributions. You eat some hors d'oeuvres and leave.

BELONGING AT WORK

From an organizational perspective, belonging is achieved when three specific attributes are present: inclusion, connection, and purpose. Inclusion, as we have seen, occurs when people feel respected and valued, when they are invited and encouraged to participate, and when they feel that those around them appreciate their contributions, perspectives, and opinions. Connection happens when people are able to form meaningful bonds and relationships with those around them, and when they feel that those same people share their values. Purpose describes the sense that your work matters and that the effort you put in is going toward a worthwhile goal or outcome.*

Belonging must happen organically. You cannot manufacture it or "strategize" it into existence. That said, you can—and should—proactively work to foster a sense of belonging using many of the same techniques we've discussed in this book. Reverse mentoring works by removing the barriers that often exist between people, particularly

---

* Jeff Schwartz, David Mallon, Yves Van Durme, Maren Hauptmann, Ramona Yan, and Shannon Poynton, "The Social Enterprise at Work: Paradox as a Path Forward," Introduction to "2020 Global Human Capital Trends," *Deloitte Insights*, May 15, 2020, https://www2.deloitte.com/us/en/insights/focus/human -capital-trends/2020/technology-and-the-social-enterprise.html.

people who come from different backgrounds. By encouraging individuals to share their stories, you allow them to chip away at those barriers, to explore their commonalities, and to understand their differences. On a one-on-one level, this creates connection, empathy, and a will toward personal growth and change. On an organizational level, it creates belonging.

Research shows that cultures that prioritize storytelling, that give employees the space to share their experiences without fear of judgment or reprisal, have a stronger sense of belonging than those that don't allow for such personal connection. At times, this sort of openness can create conflict and dissent, which is why we so often avoid it. Many organizations would prefer to take the path of least resistance, but those paths rarely lead to remarkable destinations. Think of Dorothy in *The Wizard of Oz* or Frodo from *The Lord of the Rings*. In order to fulfill their destinies, they had to confront all sorts of trials and tribulations, ones they could have easily avoided if they'd stayed at home in bed. But the outcome was worth it.

When people feel safe bringing their whole selves to work, they don't need to waste energy trying to perform as someone they're not or obsess over how people perceive them. They can perform their jobs with ease, not simply comfortable in their identity but empowered by the knowledge that their colleagues value and respect them for their unique talents, skills, perspectives, and ideas.

Michelle described acclimatizing to the culture of her new organization, an international creative agency that, judging by the external advertisements and recruitment campaigns, seemed very inclusive.

When I first started working there, I didn't realize that part of the company culture was that people often showed up late to meetings. I am a naturally punctual person, so in my first week, I was the first person to arrive to a few team meetings. On not one but *three* occasions, when my (mostly white) colleagues arrived, they mistook me (a Black woman) for a member of the catering staff. There's nothing offensive about being mistaken for a service worker, but the incidents reminded me that I was inherently different, that my colleagues were not used to working with people who looked like me and had been quick to assume that I did not belong in the room. As a result, I felt like I didn't belong—even though I had the same qualifications, experience, and skills as they did.

It wasn't until I agreed to be a mentor to the company CEO that I started to see the power in sharing these experiences and my own story. In having the opportunity to educate someone, to have them really listen and understand my perspectives, I felt hopeful about the organization and empowered as an employee. I felt like I belonged.

As you move forward with your reverse mentoring program, consider how you can harness the power of storytelling beyond the confines of the mentor-mentee relationship so it becomes a part of your everyday culture. Imagine what it might look like if the same spirit of safety, trust, openness, and curiosity that existed in your mentoring relationships existed in all corners of your organization. How would it function? How would people relate to one another? How would people feel to show up to work there? What might you be able to accomplish?

This might seem like pie-in-the-sky dreaming, but that's only because we have very few examples of what this looks like in reality. For so long, we've accepted the idea that the workplace is simply that—a place of work and nothing more. Employees exist to do a job, and anything that "gets in the way" of that job—like emotion or stress or personal needs—is a distraction that should be ignored. But we do not clock out of being human when we clock in for the day. To deny our needs, frustrations, desires, and quirks as human beings is to deny reality, and—as any great leader would tell you—denying reality is a sure way to become irrelevant very quickly.

You already have what you need to create a culture of belonging at your organization. There is a power in our stories, and we all have stories to tell. Research has shown that learning and interest is piqued when stories are told, when individuals share situations, feelings, and transformations. The realness is acknowledging some biases that you perhaps came to the table with, that aha moment, and your commitment to action and change. This is the value of a powerful story. The values of authenticity and vulnerability are essential for a transformative reverse mentoring experience, and they are also key to telling a compelling story. How will you tell yours?

Reverse mentoring is still a relatively new tool in the drive to promote more inclusion and belonging in the workplace. As such, it's important for us to share our stories and to continue to learn about what makes for an effective program—and what will set us up to fail.

To learn more about reverse mentoring, find out how to set up your own reverse mentoring program, and/or share your story as a mentor or mentee, reach out to me through any of the following channels. I'd love to hear from you!

Email: Hello@eminere.co.uk
LinkedIn.com/in/patricegordon
Instagram: @the_patrice_g
Twitter: @ThePatriceG

Acknowledgments

Thanking God for lighting my path along the way and the serendipity of life that led me to write this book.

A special thanks to my mother who has instilled hope and faith in me since my first breath. Thank you for all your sacrifices.

Hayley, who saw a light in me and encouraged me to shine brighter, I will forever be grateful for you.

To my Family and Tribe—thank you for your endless support: Anna, Bridget, Chalene, Carolyn, Dionyse, Hanae, Issy, Judolene, Kay, Natasha, Pauline, Rupi, Sasha, Sonia, Sumati, Susan, Syrita.

To my Virgin family—Craig, Estelle, Juha, Shai, Jackie, Charlotte, Sir Richard Branson, and Holly Branson—thank you for listening and allowing me to contribute toward the legacy at Virgin and live out my true purpose in life.

TED and Brene Brown who gave me the platform to amplify my stories.

To those who have worked with me to make this all possible, Brooke, Mark, Dan, and Tom.

Optimum est alius nondum venit.